Endorsements

Most people get into "sales" because they want to make a lot of money and/or control their own time. But, very few ever earn the income they dreamed of because they never "get it."

Steve A Klein wasn't a "born salesman" when I met him over twenty years ago. However, he was bright, followed directions well, was committed to high achievement, and learned quickly. Because he learned how to become successful in sales . . . he is able to now share success requirements with you in a way you can understand and put to use for your success.

Sell When You See the Whites of Their Eyes! is the result of over twenty years of personal sales success and Steve's determination to "Earn four times as much money in one-fourth the time." He has been able to accomplish this goal because he understands the incredible power of mental attitude, results tracking, and the continuity of the selling process.

Many books are written with a little knowledge and a lot of theory. Steve has the respect of everyone who has watched his progressive success. He has written this book as a celebration of his success and his desire to share these skills with you. "Steve's stuff" works in every line of sales.

If you were to read only one "sales" book in your lifetime and expect to learn the "art" of selling, you are holding that book in your hands right now.

Steve "got it" and now . . . you can, too.

> Ben Bellus, Managing General Agent
> American Income Life Insurance Company

Great athletes are diligent in their preparation. Steve Klein is no less diligent in his preparation as a great salesperson.

I had the privilege of managing Steve early in his career, and I assure the reader of this book that the contents are based on thousands of hours of study, preparation, fact-finding, and face-to-face sales presentations.

This is an opportunity to advance your sales career by learning from a truly professional salesperson.

> Bill Cochran
> Business Owner

I'm sure you'll find this a fun and enlightening read. Steve has the rare quality of building word pictures that allow readers and audiences to get to the heart of his message and greatly benefit from his knowledge and extensive life experience. A wonderful storyteller . . . enjoy.

Richard Resare, General Partner
ShowMax Marketing, L.P.

I have known Steve Klein for almost twenty years. During this time, I watched him become successful by developing sales processes and tracking the results. His positive attitude during challenging times as well as good times has made him a consistent winner. Thank you, Steve, for putting this into writing.

Dale Ware
Business Owner

Steve Klein is an enthusiastic and effective teacher. His book, *Sell When You See the Whites of Their Eyes!* is a must read for anyone in sales who is seeking to improve their skills.

Mike Postlewait, President
Management By Strengths, Inc.

Steve's formula for successful selling combines the best sales skills with practical sales strategies. It's a winning approach sure to be embraced by new and seasoned sales professionals.

Barbara Gilbert, Strategic Development Manager
The Dallas Morning News

SELL

When You See the Whites of Their Eyes!

SELL

When You See the
Whites of Their Eyes!

Steve A Klein

BROWN BOOKS

Dallas, Texas

For information, please contact Brown Books
16200 North Dallas Parkway, Suite 225
Dallas, Texas 75248
972-381-0009

First Printing, 2002
ISBN 0-9711928-0-4
LCCN 2002090385

BROWN BOOKS
www.brownbooks.com

DEDICATION

This book is dedicated to my father, S. Robert Klein. He's the salesman's salesman.

My father has been a salesman all of his life. He's always selling . . . if not his product or service, at least himself. Years ago, I must have internalized much of what my father knew about selling. Apparently, I picked up his philosophy and attitudes unconsciously. But I never wanted to be a salesman!

Thirty days after beginning my first job out of college, as a one-man news staff/news director at a small radio station in Nebraska, my boss took me out for a cup of coffee. After a few minutes of small talk, he fired me.

As I sat across from him, stunned, he asked if I would like to become a salesman. He told me that I could trade jobs with the current salesman and that the other fellow would become the news director. Apparently, my boss had seen potential in me that I wasn't aware of. He said I'd receive the same pay per month plus ten percent commission.

I accepted on the spot. The decision was purely economical. I had just moved 500 miles from home, and it was the only job offer I had had that morning. He told me to be at his office after lunch, and he would give me what I needed to sell.

I assumed we'd begin with some sort of sales training. Instead, when I arrived, he gave me a rate card, a list of clients that had previously purchased advertising, and said, "Go get 'em."

My first sales presentation was, "You don't want to buy any advertising, do you?" I was acknowledged with agreement. "Yes, you're right. I don't want to buy any advertising!" And so my sales career began.

Surprisingly, a few clients began to buy. But the turning point came during a local Chamber of Commerce luncheon, with a gubernatorial candidate as the featured speaker. I have no recollection of the content of his message, but I remember the feeling I had after his talk. He was the first person I had ever heard who actually inspired me to take action to change my life!

I ran out of that meeting to see my next prospect. This retailer had previously purchased advertising long ago, had a bad experience, and had vowed never to advertise with us again. He and I had become friends, though he still wouldn't buy advertising from me. I ran into his store, excitedly told him about a current radio promotion we had, and he said yes! A few weeks later, I asked him why, after all this time, he finally bought! He said that my enthusiasm was so great; he was afraid not to!

The rest, as they say, is history, and the result is this book.

Dad, thanks for giving me the insight, the enthusiasm, and the right attitude to make this book possible.

TABLE OF CONTENTS

DEDICATION   VII

INTRODUCTION   XIII

ACKNOWLEDGMENTS   XV

THE SALESMAN'S FABLE   1

PART ONE: **ATTITUDE**   7

Results   7

Skills/Activity/Attitude   13

Confidence   15

The Power of Magnetism   19

Belief   22

PART TWO: **TRACKING STEPS TO SUCCESS!**   25

1) Objectives   25

2) Objective Folders   29

3) Chart of Accounts   31

4) Business Accounts   34

5) Self-Management   36

6) High-Payout Activities   39

7) The Self-Management System   41

8) Focus on the "Important"   43

9) Daily Sales Activities   47

10) Success Target   49

11) Correct, Consistent, Daily Checklist—Scorekeeping   51

12) Success Checklist   60

13) MRO Chart   63

PART THREE: **THE NINE-STEP SALES PROCESS**   67

Process   69

Prospect Agreement   71

     "Set expectations"   72

     "Do what you say you will do"   73

     "Gain agreement"   73

PROCESS STEP NO. 1: THE CONTACT — SETTING THE MEETING   75

PROCESS STEP NO. 2: THE MEETING — REMOVING THE "GARBAGE CAN LID"   82

PROCESS STEP NO. 3: THE INTERVIEW — FINDING THE "GAP"   86

     Qualifying the Prospect   89

     The Gap   94

     Owning Your Prospect's Problems   96

Client Motivation   98
PROCESS STEP NO. 4: THE PRESENTATION — CLOSING THE "GAP"   100
Facilitation   103
PROCESS STEP NO. 5: THE NEGOTIATION   105
Always Negotiate on Something   108
PROCESS STEP NO. 6: THE REASSURANCE — HANDLING OBJECTIONS   110
PROCESS STEP NO. 7: THE DELIVERY   114
PROCESS STEP NO. 8: THE NEW PROSPECT — GETTING REFERRALS   117
Referrals   118
Centers of Influence   122
Speaking Engagements   123
Direct Mail   125
Cold Calling   128
Eight Additional Successful Prospecting Methods   130
PROCESS STEP NO. 9: THE FOLLOW-UP — RELATIONSHIP MANAGEMENT   133
Repetition Through Persistence   138
The Follow-Up System   142
Sales No. 1-9   145
Salesperson vs. Sales Consultant   147

PART FOUR: **CONDITIONING CHANGE FOR RESULTS**   151
A Conditioning Fable   151
Comfort Zone   154
Habit   157
Insanity   159
Developing the Larger Comfort Zone   161
Ninety Days Same as Change   164
Tenth Multiple   167
Next   170
Attitudes/Activities/Skills   172
Success Degrees   174
Passion   179
Risking   181
Commitment   184
The "Slight Edge"   186
18 Keys to Remember During the Critical Sales Confrontation   190
"It's in Your Hands" Fable   194

Appendix   195
1) Chart of Accounts   197
2) Business Accounts   199
3) Weekly Planning Guide   201

4) Daily Sales Activities   203

5) Correct, Consistent Daily Activity—Scorekeeping   205

6) CCDA Ratios   207

7) Success Checklist   209

8) MRO Chart   211

Order Form   213

Author's Biography   215

INTRODUCTION

The master in the art of living makes little distinction between
his work and his play, his labors and his leisure, his mind and his body,
his information and his recreation, his love and his religion. He
hardly knows which is which. He simply pursues his vision of excellence at
whatever he does, leaving others to decide whether he is working
or playing. To him he's always doing both.

∿ JAMES MICHENER

Hundreds of books have been written about the subject of sales. Although I haven't read anywhere near all of them, I've read my fair share, and I must say that I have never read a book about selling that didn't either increase my sales through the use of new techniques or help me to understand my prospect better.

To help you understand why I've written yet another book about this subject, I'll begin by telling you what not to expect. This isn't a book about techniques. Most work quite well, but most salespeople don't think of techniques while they're with their prospect; they're thinking about how to assist their prospect.

Why are some salespeople more successful than other salespeople? Why do some salespeople continually outsell their competitors? Great salespeople enter every presentation knowing the sales techniques and using them when appropriate, while focusing on the prospect. And that's what this book is all about.

We're in a new sales world today. Focusing on the prospect or client is not new. But increased competition and the number of similar products and services on the market confuse prospects, and they need more assistance today than they did in the past.

And that's where today's salesperson steps in. The high-income salesperson of today focuses on the prospect. It's not that you don't need the other books and information about sales, but today's salesperson needs to build on that foundation with relationship building.

Sell When You See the Whites of Their Eyes! focuses on relationships with prospects and clients. Successful relationships involve trust. This will be a theme throughout this book. In addition, you'll understand how to direct your attitudes toward achieving results that you want to achieve, while developing methods of tracking your sales activities so that the trust relationship with your prospect and client becomes paramount to the sale.

To help you understand how you develop that trust, the art of questioning is the key to the sales process steps in Part III. By breaking apart the sales process and dissecting each part, you'll have a better understanding of how and why your prospect buys.

Sell When You See the Whites of Their Eyes! will move you to the upper echelons of sales success. Follow the "Actions" after each section and you'll realize how easy selling truly is.

ACKNOWLEDGMENTS

Books are never written in a vacuum. An author's insight and information are generally gleaned from years of learning, succeeding and failing at any number of pursuits. Individuals and experiences add to this insight.

This book was written as a result of experiences, interactions and sales presentations made over the last twenty-seven years. Ideas were picked up, absorbed, used, and internalized over that time.

Correct acknowledgments may be inconsistent, or possibly even omitted. Please accept my apologies if this has occurred. The intent of this writing is to be as accurate as possible. Any corrections should be brought to the author's attention and will be corrected in any future printings.

Sell When You See the Whites of Their Eyes!

It is not the strongest of the species that survive,
nor the most intelligent, but the one most responsive to change.
∾ CHARLES DARWIN

Sell When You See the Whites of Their Eyes!

THE SALESMAN'S FABLE

And in those days, behold, there came through the gates of the city
a salesman from afar, and it came to pass that he sold plenty.
And in that city were they that were order takers and they that
spent their days in adding to the alibi sheets. Mightily
were they astonished. They said one to the other, "How doth he
getteth away with it?" And it came to pass that many were
gathered in the back office, and a soothsayer came among them.
And he was one wise guy. And they spoke and questioned
him saying, "How is it that this stranger accomplisheth the impossible?"
Whereupon the soothsayer made answer, "He of whom you speak
is one hustler. He ariseth in the morning and goeth forth full of pep.
He complaineth not neither doth he know despair. He is arrayed in
purple and fine linen, while ye go forth with pants unpressed.
"While ye gather here and say one to the other, 'Verily this is a terrible
day to work,' he is already abroad. And when the eleventh hour
cometh, he needeth no alibi. He knoweth his line and they that would
stave him off, they give him orders. Men they say unto him
'nay' when he cometh in, yet when he goeth forth he hath their
names on the line that is dotted.
'He taketh with him the two angels' 'inspiration' and 'perspiration'
and worketh to beat hell. Verily I say unto you, go and do likewise."
∾ AUTHOR UNKNOWN

1

Are you that salesman? Are you able to develop large numbers of clients who continually buy from you because you can "see the whites of their eyes?"

A colleague of mine, Mike Postlewait, owns Management By Strengths, a training company in Olathe, Kansas, that teaches individuals how to understand temperaments. His philosophy is that the better you understand yourself and others, the better you can work with and sell to others.

Within that training, Mike uses the following example about being out of control:

"You are standing in an alley, and a guy is walking toward you. Immediately, you realize this guy is not friendly because he is throwing rocks at you as he walks toward you. You look for a way out of the alley and see there is no way out, but you notice a garbage can lid (the shield) and start deflecting the rocks."

Mike continues, "It's the same with our psyche—if something goes against your temperament, you become defensive and raise that shield, then it is difficult to receive what is being said."

Hence the title of this book, *Sell When You See the Whites of Their Eyes!* The only way to sell, the only way to develop a relationship with your prospect, and the only way to develop referrals and repeat business is for you to get your prospect to pull down that "garbage can lid" (the shield) and get to understand your prospect.

What does seeing the "whites of their eyes" mean? I can only get close to you (psychologically) and possibly intimate with you (meaning you've opened up to me) if I can see your eyes. This is the ability to communicate with and get inside the mind of the other person. If I were to stand about ten feet away from you and attempt to conduct a conversation, I wouldn't be able to effectively communicate, since I wouldn't be able to watch your expressions and facial movements. I would be too far away.

But you won't let me get that close if you don't trust me or feel that I care about you. When I've proven to you that I do care and that you can trust me, you begin to have confidence in me and let me get close enough to see the "whites of your eyes!"

The "garbage can lid" Mike refers to is the shield your prospect puts up until you get close enough to them that they pull it down. You can't pull the shield down yourself, only your prospect will pull it down, based on how you interact with them. Your prospect puts the "garbage can lid" down when they feel that you care about them. And they feel you care about them when you begin to help solve their problems, not yours.

"Garbage can lids" or shields can be anything your prospect or client uses as a way to keep you at a distance. People have developed an innate distrust of anything new, especially if they are the ones who say "yes" first. They use these shields to keep you at bay. Their thinking is "if you can't get close to me, I won't have to make a decision to buy right now."

"Garbage can lids" may be verbal and may include statements like these:

"I only have a few minutes."
"I never buy anything right away."
"I have to talk to my partner (spouse, associate) first."
"Just looking (retail)."
"I need more information."

Do statements like these indicate that your prospect won't buy from you? Absolutely not! Your job is to get close enough to your prospect for them to pull these "shields" down and turn this individual into a loyal and repeat client.

Sell When You See the Whites of Their Eyes! will show you how to help your prospect pull their "lids" down by helping you to understand yourself. You can't change others. You can only change yourself; and by changing your approach to your prospects, your prospects will change toward you, pull down that "lid" and become your client.

Sell When You See the Whites of Their Eyes! is broken into four sections. Section one will show you what attitudes to develop to begin the change process. Section two will help you develop methods to track and organize your sales activity.

The third section is the heart of this book. Here, you'll begin to understand the sales process and make it work to your advantage by learning how to help your prospect pull their shield down.

And finally, section four will help you develop additional attitudes and behaviors necessary to make the changes you've planned.

You'll notice that two references are used throughout this book. These terms are "prospect" and "client." If you haven't yet sold someone or some entity, they remain a "prospect" until sold. Even after the sale, the "client" may again be a "prospect" because they once again can be sold.

Once your "prospect" buys, he or she becomes a "client" rather than a "customer." The term "customer" connotes someone who may or may not buy again from you. The attitude throughout this book is to make your new "client" someone who continually wants what you're selling. Therefore, "client" is used as a term to better describe the relationship you develop by applying the ideas and actions suggested throughout this book.

You'll also see the following action steps designed to help guide you through the steps to develop your sales plan. The format of this book is designed to let you write your thoughts and ideas in such a way as to develop this success plan to achieve your results and acquire more clients.

Schedule time each day to work on one or two action steps throughout this book. Your maximum benefit will come from a minimum of thirty minutes. It's always better to spread your time over the course of a week. It's much like exercise. The true benefit comes from a daily regimen rather than being a weekend warrior.

Use this book as a workbook. When you find something that is important to you, underline, highlight or use a notebook to take notes. This information will then be readily available for your review. Time invested in reviewing what you'd like to learn and change pays dividends. Follow through on each action step. By the time you arrive at the end, you'll have a well-formulated plan to achieve the results you'll begin to establish in the first section.

You may also want to get a notebook or pad of paper and graph paper. Many action steps instruct you to put a large amount of information on paper. Rather than take up space in this book, you can begin to develop your own plan in your own book.

By developing these action steps, you'll be thinking outside of your normal mindset, so you can look at another way to operate your business. You may not agree with some of the ideas and suggestions, but you'll be comparing your way against another.

To achieve success, the kind of success you really would like to have, takes courage! Before you can achieve this kind of success, you need to earn the right to have your success. By developing the action steps throughout this book and putting them into action, you'll begin to take the steps necessary to earn this right and earn the success you deserve.

How many ways are there to sell? As many ways as there are salespeople. You're only limited by your own imagination. Use your imagination as you read this book and when you write down your thoughts in the action steps. The only thing that might change is your sales success!

The money you make in any line of endeavor is determined
12½ percent by knowledge and 87½ percent by your ability to deal with people.
❧ STANFORD UNIVERSITY INSTITUTE

Action: What are those "garbage can lids" that your prospects are putting up? List as many as you can before continuing.

1. _____

_____

2. _____

_____

3. _____

_____

4. _____

_____

5. _____

_____

Sell When You See the Whites of Their Eyes!

PART ONE:

Attitude

RESULTS

If you care enough for a result you will most certainly attain it.
∾ WILLIAM JAMES

Let's begin to get close to your prospect and "see the whites of their eyes" by focusing on the results you'd like to attain.

The number one reason why salespeople do not achieve the results they are attempting to achieve is because they don't know what they want those results to be!

We've all heard about goals, objectives and dreams. Let's focus on the term "results" because everyone has them. Good, bad or mediocre, we all get results. Let's begin to control them and help our prospects pull their shields down.

A client once told me the story about the "Merlin Concept." Merlin, if you'll remember from history and stories, was King Arthur's confidant, mentor, and magician. Arthur would use him as his sounding board whenever problems and decisions overwhelmed him. Whenever Merlin gave Arthur advice, it came true. Arthur asked Merlin how he was able to predict the future so accurately.

"It's not difficult," Merlin said. "I'm living my life backwards, and I've already experienced the exact scenes I've described."

Be like Merlin. Live your life backwards. See your life exactly as you'd like it to be. Now use the "Merlin Concept" and work backwards to today, seeing exactly what you'll have to do to be at some point in the future.

The best way to predict the future is to create it.
∾ PETER DRUCKER

Let's take income as an example. You want to make $100,000 next year. With two weeks' vacation, that's broken down into $2,000 each week, or $400 per day. What will you have to do to make $400 every day? This is the activity level that you'll need to accomplish daily. You've now worked backwards from your end result.

If you'd like to make one sale per day,

a) How many prospects are you going to have to ask to buy daily to make one sale?

b) How many presentations will you have to make to be able to ask them to buy?

c) How many appointments will you have to make to be able to see that number of prospects?

d) How many people will you have to talk to daily to set up those appointments?

e) How many referrals will you need on a daily basis to be able to speak with that number of people?

The secret of success is constancy to purpose.
∾ BENJAMIN DISRAELI

Now that you've made a decision to focus on specific results, it's necessary to begin to establish correct actions and habits to follow-through on your steps to success. No matter what we do for a living, we all eventually get off track. We begin by letting things we have no control over, such as distractions, get in our way. We are no longer in control of ourselves; everything and everyone else is now controlling us. Don't let this continue to happen to you. Take your life back! Don't let these outside distractions control your success.

Again, you first need to determine what you want your results to be. These results will control your behavior which, in turn, affects your attitude, which allows outside information to impact you. The model looks like this:

Results › Behavior › Attitudes › Information

Your **Results** determine your **Behavior** (the way you act), which influences your **Attitudes** (the way you think), which allows **Information** to control you.

But if you first decide what results you want in your life, or at least through next year, then you can control what information affects your attitude and behavior to get the results you've been focused on.

Information › Attitudes › Behavior › Results

Now the **Information** you choose impacts your **Attitudes** (the way you think), which controls your **Behavior** (your actions), which gives you the **Results** you want. (SUCCESS MOTIVATION INSTITUTE, WACO, TX)

Let's use two examples of how this model might work. You arrive home after a long day, turn on the evening news and hear that there's a major recession coming to your area. You keep hearing this information repeatedly for the next week. Will this affect your attitude? Will it impact your behavior? Will it affect your results?

Next scenario: Your boss tells you that no matter what happens this year (assuming you do your work), your income will double over last year. You hear your income will double over and over, and you believe it. Will this information from your boss have an impact on your attitude? Will it control your behavior? And will you get better results?

Even though both of these examples have opposite outcomes, they're actually similar. Without specific results to focus on, outside information controls your outcome. Now, if my boss is going to double my income, I'll sure let that affect me. But, in most cases, the situations and circumstances surrounding them control most salespeople. Decide today exactly what you want your results to be, and then look for the information necessary to get those results. If you don't, the information that's out there will control you.

If you do not develop a strategy of your own, you become a part of someone else's strategy. You, in fact, become reactive to external circumstances. The absence of strategy is fine if you don't care where you're going.

༄ ALVIN TOFFLER

Where do you find the information necessary to achieve your results? Interestingly, it begins to show up once you begin to focus on the results. For instance, let's say you decide the number one result you'd like to accomplish this year is to buy a specific automobile.

First, go to the dealership that has the automobile you're interested in. Find the right car, the right style, and the right color. Get into it, feel it, touch it, test-drive it. After the test-drive, hand the salesperson the camera you brought with you and have the salesperson take a picture of *your* new automobile. Then, make multiple copies of the picture and put it everywhere you are during the day: your car, on your bathroom mirror, in your wallet or purse, and at your desk.

What you're doing is inundating your subconscious mind with new information without thinking about it. After a while, your conscious mind doesn't know the difference between what's real and what isn't. Your subconscious believes you already have the car, and it causes you to do the things necessary to get your new automobile.

Here's an example: Two friends are talking about wealth. The first one says that he would like enough money to buy an elephant. "Why do you want to buy an elephant?" his friend asked. "I don't want to *buy* an elephant. I just want enough *money* to buy an elephant."

And this is what your mind will do for you. Since your subconscious mind believes you already have this car, it causes you to act in such a way that your actions help you find ways to have your new car. But money may not be the only way to accomplish your results.

There's an urban legend of the fellow who was looking for a late-model Mercedes. He'd scour the classifieds every morning looking for an inexpensive version of this car.

Then one morning he sees this one being offered for just $100. Believing it is a misprint, he calls the number to find the true price of the vehicle. A woman answers and tells him that $100 is the actual price of the car.

"What's wrong with it," he asks. "Nothing," replies the woman. "I have to see this car," says the fellow as he hangs up to drive over and see the car.

When he arrives at the woman's home, he looks the car over and knocks on the door. The woman comes out, hands him the keys and they go for a test-drive. Nothing is wrong with the car. Deciding he could take the chance, he hands the woman $100 and receives the title to the car.

"Now that I own this vehicle," says the fellow, "why did you just sell it for $100?"

The woman answers, "My husband just ran off with his secretary," she says. "He called the other night and asked me to sell the Mercedes . . . and send him the proceeds!"

This is how your subconscious mind works. Focus on your result long enough and your mind leads you to whatever you're focused on.

Actually, the most effective generator of ideas for your subconscious mind is probably on your desk right now. It's a sticky note. Write a result you are attempting to achieve on a number of notes and stick them everywhere you put the picture of the automobile. You can write a dollar figure, draw a small picture or write a word. It doesn't matter what it is because your subconscious mind is working for you all of the time and will begin to help you do the things necessary to get that result.

During my years with a sales force, we put our objective on a sign above every door going in and out of the office. After awhile, nobody really consciously noticed the numbers, but they did subconsciously, and we hit the numbers more often than not because we had that secret weapon working for us.

So how important is it to develop results? It's the difference between succeeding and failing. Once you have the results nailed down specifically, your mind begins to develop ideas to change the way you think. Once your thinking changes, you begin to act differently. And once your actions change, you begin to achieve the results you're focused on.

But there's an important element to keep in mind. The commitment you have toward the results you are attempting to accomplish has to be tremendously strong. This is an attitude that moves you along the path to achievement.

If you work toward a result half-heartedly knowing you probably will never achieve the result, you're also setting yourself up for future failure. If you knock yourself out working toward achieving your objective, you're setting yourself up for future success.

But what happens when you absolutely move heaven and earth as you work toward your result, but fall short? Does this set up another failure cycle in the future?

Absolutely not. Your subconscious mind works on the premise that you have already achieved the result you've set out for before you achieve it, assuming you believe you'll achieve it before you start. So all your mind is doing is putting into place exactly what you need to do to make it happen. Your subconscious mind simply sees this as a temporary setback and not a permanent failure.

Therefore, working as hard as you can and not accomplishing your result is almost as good as accomplishing what you want, as far as your subconscious is concerned. The fact that you did everything you could is still setting yourself up for success in the future. Your future is decided by what you decide today, as long as you don't quit and give up.

What's occurring is a process of 'mental osmosis.' The pictured ideas of what you want sinks into your subconscious. Then you will have it because it has you.

ꙮ NORMAN V. PEALE

Action: Even though we'll discuss these questions again during Part II, answer the questions above by writing down a number for each of the following (examples in parenthesis):

Next year's income: _____

Weekly income (divide by 50): _____

Daily income: (divide by 5): _____

No. of Presentations you'd like to make daily (4): _____

No. of Appointments you'd like to book daily (5): _____

No. of Prospects you'd like to ask for Appointments daily (15):_____

No. of Referrals you'd like to receive daily (20): _____

SKILLS/ACTIVITY/ATTITUDE

Spectacular success is always preceded by unspectacular preparation.

∾ AUTHOR UNKNOWN

Salespeople continually focus on improving their selling skills. The problem with having great skills is they are useless without the correct activity and attitudes. Salespeople focus on:

1) Improving their selling skills, then
2) Increasing their selling activity, and then
3) Working on their attitudes.

But this is backwards. Let's say a salesperson is having a hard time closing a sale. Working on closing skills does them very little good if their activity level of presentations is low and their attitude about selling is poor.

A salesperson needs to:

1) First, focus on your mental attitude. Begin to develop results and objectives for where you want to be in the future. See yourself accomplishing both the results you want and the results your clients will receive from doing business with you.
2) Next, focus on your level of activity. Activity is second because this activity level will not increase unless your attitude is correct. It's difficult to see more prospects and make more presentations if you're not thinking clearly. It can be done, but it is difficult. Here's where you're developing your activity game plan and sticking to it. How many calls will you make each day? How many prospects will you see each day? How many new referrals will you receive from every prospect?

    You'll notice that these activities are ones we have control over. A salesperson has little control over the number of sales he/she makes. But the salesperson has total control over the amount of raw activity performed daily. Your attitude will improve when you achieve your activity results daily. To improve even more, overachieve on your activity level.
3) Finally, work on your skill level. Interestingly, you won't have to spend much time here. By developing the right attitudes about your selling activities and increasing the level of activity, your skills will increase. This is not to say that

you shouldn't continually take courses and read books about various aspects of your sales career. You should invest in yourself on a regular basis. But by accomplishing the first two areas before working on your skills, these will generally take care of themselves.

Many salespeople wait to see their prospects until they have honed their sales skills. I've always wondered how they do that, because they aren't seeing any live prospects and they aren't making any money! Skills are honed by doing. The best "doing" is seeing your prospects and learning from live situations.

Knowing is not enough, we must apply. Willing is not enough, we must do.

∾ GOETHE

Action: What attitudes do you have about selling and/or your career that may need a little tweaking? These are the attitudes that need to change before your activity will increase and your skills will improve. Write those down and begin to increase your activity and skills:

1. _____

_____

2. _____

_____

3. _____

_____

4. _____

_____

5. _____

_____

CONFIDENCE

*Confidence is entering a sales contest and wondering
who's going to come in second!*
∞ AUTHOR UNKNOWN

As a salesperson with the motivation to succeed, you are never competing with anyone but yourself.

The first year I worked for a major training company, my objective was to be rookie-of-the-year. My motivation was high, since the first year is the only year you can win the award. At the first awards convention I attended, I asked the current rookie-of-the-year winner if he would take my picture holding his award. He agreed, and I kept that picture in front of me all year.

Toward the end of the year, I was neck-and-neck with another distributor. My marketing director's assistant told me that the other distributor had a record day the previous day. When I heard that news, I fell flat on my face and couldn't sell a thing. This was because I let something I had no control over control me.

Remember, no matter what happens in life, the only control you have is over yourself and no one else. Whenever you're in a sales contest, remember only you have control. What's interesting is that in a race with ninety-nine other salespeople, only about three of you understand this phenomenon. As a result, ninety-seven salespeople are continually worried about what everyone else is doing. This situation takes up so much energy and effort that they lose sight of what they need to be doing.

Only three percent, or three salespeople, understand this situation. In a contest with ninety-nine others, you actually are only competing with two other individuals. With all skill levels being equal, the salesperson with the right attitude about controlling themselves generally wins. In every sales contest I've won, others had more skill and abilities than I had. The only difference was that I entered the sales contest with the 100 percent belief that I had already won. That attitude and the persistence to stay with my activity level gained me the upper hand and the number one position.

How did I develop that belief and persistence to continue my activity no matter what? The story of the "Robot" will help you understand.

THE ROBOT

I have a little robot that goes around with me.
I tell it what I'm thinking. I tell it what I see.
I tell my little robot all my hopes and fears.
It listens and remembers everything it hears.

At first my little robot followed my command.
But after years of training, it's gotten out of hand.
It doesn't care what's right or wrong, or what is false or true.
No matter how I try now, it tells me what to do!

∾ AUTHOR UNKNOWN

Our subconscious mind is our "Robot." This "Robot" believes what we tell it on a regular basis. For instance, let's say you believe you can't remember names and that you have a poor memory. You keep feeding your subconscious mind, or robot, this information over and over.

One day you go to an important meeting and decide that you will remember every person you meet. After meeting the third person, you realize you have forgotten the names of the first two individuals. What happened? You programmed your robot so many times that it activated the command to forget names even though consciously you told your mind to remember them. "I just did what you've been telling me to do," says the robot. It's very difficult to re-program something that's been preprogrammed for so long.

I regularly read and repeat specific statements to myself everyday. Since I'm not a totally positive person by nature, it's even more important that I continually program myself to become the person I want to become in order to reach my objectives.

These are simply verbal statements telling you what and where you're to be or become. There are three ways I've used verbal statements effectively:

1) Every morning as I awake, I repeat a statement to myself to get the morning started correctly. The hardest thing I do all day is to physically get myself out of bed in the morning, so this statement (taken from something I read long ago) is what gets my motor cranked in the morning. (By the way, once you use an affirmation over and over again, you own it, because it's yours.)

This is a new day. God has given me this day to use, as I will. I can waste it or use it for good. What I do today is important because I'm exchanging a day of my life for it. When tomorrow comes this day will be gone forever leaving in its place something I've traded for it. I want it to be gain, not loss; good, not evil; success not failure, in order that I will not regret the price I've paid for it.
ɔ AUTHOR UNKNOWN

2) As I prepare for my day during my daily prep time, I read aloud four pages of statements I've written for myself. These statements start me thinking clearly.

3) In addition, I listen to a self-recorded twenty-minute tape each morning, to continue my focus on my objectives.

When water drips on a stone, over time, it begins to wear away the stone. This is what these statements have accomplished. Over the years, my attitude has been changed and altered by the ideas I think are important. I decided that I was going to allow only certain information to remain in my head. This process keeps it clear.

A study has shown that two-thirds of a message read or heard only once is forgotten within twenty-four hours and is practically out of mind within thirty days. A message read or heard several times a day for eight days is virtually memorized. At the end of thirty days, the memory retains 90 percent of the message. This is why it's imperative to make sure you keep putting the information you want into your head on a regular basis.

Repetition is the mother of learning.
ɔ AUTHOR UNKNOWN

Action No. 1: Write five statements right now about where you'd like to be. Remember to make them personal, present tense, positive, colorful and fun!

1. _____

_____

2. _____

_____

3. _____

_____

4. _____

_____

5. _____

_____

Action No. 2: One way to achieve your objectives is to set aside time for self-development. One half-hour each day is almost two-hundred hours per year of learning. By doing this, you can improve tremendously. Write down when you'll use your study time each day: _____

THE POWER OF MAGNETISM

It's easier to get where you'd like to be if you dress like you're already there.
∾ NEWSPAPER SLOGAN FOR LEO'S MEN'S STORE, FORT WALTON BEACH, FL

The health benefits of magnets have been in the news lately. We're going to explore these benefits but from a slightly different angle. The health benefits we're going to look at are your mental success benefits.

Magnets have the power to attract. Your mind is a magnet. By focusing on what you want, you begin to attract whatever it is you've seen in your head.

Have you ever purchased an automobile and noticed after buying it that all of a sudden the same car seemed to be everywhere . . . in the same color? Or maybe you have children. Did you begin noticing more pregnant women when you or your wife became pregnant?

Like the examples above, once you begin to focus on a specific objective based on the results you're attempting to achieve, you begin the mental attraction process.

Our mind is programmed to seek whatever results we're focused on. If it's out there, we'll find it. How do you find a needle in a haystack? You have to know what the needle looks like.

Here's a personal example of how this process works when I won rookie-of-the-year. In addition to having the right attitude and looking at the rookie-of-the-year award picture every day, I also had a letter that my marketing director had sent to me. It was dated the following year and written as if I had already won the award. The letter told me how great a job I had done and even mentioned that my speech at the awards convention was electrifying. I was seeing into the future. I won that award!

During my second year, my objective became sales leader of the year. This was a fitting follow-up to rookie-of-the-year. I became so motivated to win that award that I ate, drank and slept as if I had already won. My marketing director had sent me a twelve-foot banner that said, "Congratulations, Sales Leader of the Year!"

I put that banner up near my ceiling and looked at it continually. It was always a kick when someone entered my office and congratulated me on having won that award. It was one more affirmation about how I would win. Everything I did that year was directed toward winning that award.

---

*The greater danger for most of us is not that our aim is too high
and we miss it but that it is too low and we reach it.*

∾ MICHAELANGELO

A few days into the new year, I received a call from my marketing director. He told me he had good news and bad news. He said the bad news was that I had not won Sales Leader of the Year. I was crushed! Everything I had done that year had been directed toward winning that award.

But the good news was that I had won Distributor of the Year. He told me that because I had done so well, I had outsold every other distributorship by myself. I had become number one of over five-hundred distributors across the United States. I told him that I didn't want that award, that I wanted the Sales Leader of the Year award. He said that if they were to name me Sales Leader of the Year that it would skew the entire awards program because I had done so well.

I agreed to the award, but I wanted something else. At the awards convention, when I would be named Distributor of the Year, he would also mention that I won the award by becoming the best salesperson.

Three months later, we had the awards convention. Since it was a world convention, all of the other countries received their awards first, while the United States, the host country, received their awards last. I was the last individual to receive my award before the world awards were announced.

My marketing director told everyone that I achieved the award by becoming the top salesperson. I went to the lectern, received my award, said a few words and sat down. The world awards were beginning.

As the World Sales Leader of the Year runner-up was being announced, I was thinking about how much I admired this woman and how much I would like to sell like her someday. Then they began to introduce the World Sales Leader of the Year. Halfway through the introduction I realized that they were talking about me! I had absolutely no idea I was even in the running for the award.

This is what happens when you focus visually and do the activities necessary to accomplish the result. Sometimes, you just overachieve.

A man will find that as he alters his thoughts toward things and other people, things and other people will alter toward him. Let a man radically alter his thoughts, and he will be astonished at the rapid transformation it will affect in the material conditions of his life. Men do not attract that which they want, but that which they are. The divinity that shapes our ends is in ourselves. It is our very own self. All that a man achieves is the direct result of his own thoughts. A man will only rise, conquer and achieve by lifting up his thoughts. He can only remain weak and abject and miserable by refusing to lift up his thoughts.

∾ JAMES ALLEN ("AS A MAN THINKETH")

Action: What pictures can you find that will symbolize what you want. Write down five pictures and put them in front of you to look at daily:

1. _____

_____

2. _____

_____

3. _____

_____

4. _____

_____

5. _____

_____

BELIEF

Faith means carrying on after things don't work.
∽ MOODY

The strongest human motivator we have available to us is belief. The power of belief knows that you can do something, specifically, to achieve your objectives. So how do you develop this belief? How do you develop this white-hot passion?

You begin to develop belief when you begin to see whatever it is that you want to do or achieve. When you begin to see what you want, you then begin to believe it. There are two reasons to do anything: to gain a benefit or to avoid a loss. You need to see the benefits of what you want to have. If you can't see exactly what you want to have, then it's going to be very difficult to make it happen.

See those end results, not the steps to get there. It's not, "How am I going to reach that objective?" but rather, "What objective am I going to reach?"

Obstacles are designed to keep you on track as guideposts toward your objectives. When a plane is airborne, it can easily be off track. It's kept on track because the pilot checks the instruments and stays in touch with the guides along the way. Whenever the plane gets off track (the obstacle), that causes the pilot to change direction to get on course. Obstacles keep you on track. Obstacles also make you stronger.

If you lift weights, you probably lift them to stretch your muscles. Imagine pushing your arms into the air just to say you're exercising. It wouldn't do you any good. It's the same with obstacles. These are the things that make you successful and help you grow.

You can attract what you want because your picture will create the desire to have what you want. It will help you see the end result benefit.

When you want it badly enough, you'll find a way to make it happen. That desire spells the difference between an objective and a mere wish.

If you don't have that desire strongly enough, then you don't have a true objective to shoot for. Your desire puts action into your plans. It helps you carry out those plans that you want to achieve. It's not enough just to have a plan; you need to put the "do" into the plan.

The desire to achieve develops an emotional appetite that causes you to want to have more than what you have. That desire will create the talent, and the talent will create the skills necessary, to help you get where you want to go. Those thoughts will lead to the action. The action will result in the development of the methods necessary, and the methods will create the reality of your objectives.

Faith may be defined briefly as an illogical belief
in the occurrence of the improbable.

∾ H.L. MENCKEN

Action: Do you have belief? What do you believe in? Is it you? What is it you'd like to achieve? Write down five things that you believe you'll achieve:

1. _____

_____

2. _____

_____

3. _____

_____

4. _____

_____

5. _____

_____

PART TWO

Tracking Steps to Success!

1) OBJECTIVES

Make no little plans; they have no magic to stir men's blood.
ॐ DANIEL HUDSON BURNHAM

Part I of this book focused on developing the attitudes and determining the results necessary to achieve before anything of significance will happen in your selling career. To decide what results to focus on, the development of turning dreams into an obtainable objective, is certainly the ideal beginning. Without these dreams, you won't have the ability to focus on your prospect and "see the whites of their eyes!"

Everyone dreams. We dream at night, we daydream during the day. We even fantasize about our life occasionally. Since we're doing it anyway, let's make dreaming work for us.

Your first step is to get a large pad of paper, label it "Objectives" and start writing. The mere act of putting on paper what you want begins to work on your mind and imagination.

Example number one: Put your results on paper. I was having lunch with a colleague of mine recently, and he began asking our waitress questions about her hometown, because her name badge listed the city she was from. During this conversation, she mentioned that she was going to college, and he asked her if she had any objectives. She said she had lots of them. Were they written down? "No, they're all in my head!"

Example number two: Look at your list of results to be achieved on a regular basis. A number of years ago I met with a real estate agent who worked in a "100%" office. This means that the agent, instead of splitting his commissions with his office, would keep his entire commission and pay the office a monthly rent to use their facilities. Generally, you'll find the most motivated real estate agents in these types of offices.

During our conversation, he mentioned that he hadn't had a sale in six months. For most commissioned salespeople, this is a long drought. It's even longer when you're paying a large sum of money every month to the manager of the office. I asked this agent if he had any specific objectives he wanted to achieve. He said he had a couple of dozen. I asked if he would mind showing them to me. He said not at all, and he began digging through his drawer, looking for his objectives.

After several minutes of searching, he pulled out a dog-eared piece of paper that had a number of objectives listed he wanted to achieve. I asked him if he looked at this sheet very often. He said he hadn't looked at them in six months. I asked, "Why?" And he said, "I didn't want to get discouraged about the items I wanted since I wasn't selling anything." I then asked if he thought there was any coincidence that he hadn't looked at his objectives in six months and the fact that he hadn't made a sale in six months. He didn't think there was.

Both examples show the limitations. You may feel bad that you aren't achieving your objectives, but by putting your objectives in writing, your mind works on what you put in front of it. Our mind is a mental magnet. It attracts that which it sees. How do you find a needle in a haystack? You need to first know what the needle looks like!

Another reason many people don't put their objectives in writing is that they feel that by putting them down on paper they are making a commitment that can never be changed. The words you put on paper are simply ideas, and these ideas change from moment to moment. Our mind is like the hard drive on a computer. You wouldn't think of filling your hard drive with so much data that it wouldn't be able to do any other work for you. You'd download as much information as necessary onto a floppy disk so that your hard drive would have as much freedom to do what you wanted as quickly as you wanted it to.

I've found that the more objectives you get on paper, the more you achieve. A number of years ago when I began the process of putting on paper what I wanted,

I noticed a pattern occurring each year. The first year I had written down about fifty items. I achieved about fifteen. Year number two I increased the number to a hundred and I achieved around thirty. My third year I upped the number of objectives to 150 and I ended the year with forty-five.

See the pattern? Each year I was achieving around 30 percent. And these objectives were achieved without really working too hard on them. My subconscious mind was focusing on what I wanted, and it was helping me to do what was necessary to achieve these objectives. That's the power of putting on paper those items that you want to achieve.

Since I wasn't one to fool around with my ability to achieve more than 30 percent, I decided rather than fight it, I would simply keep adding more items to my list. I not only am achieving more, but I can also predict about how much I'll achieve each year, since it's consistently around 30 percent (Your percentage may vary. The only way to find out is to keep tracking your results. More about tracking in the next section).

But here's another way this idea of getting what you want on paper can work for you. One day, prior to putting these objectives on paper, I realized that those items that I wanted to take care of in my life (my "to-do" list) were becoming overwhelming. Our mind can only think of one thing at a time, and if you're attempting to remember every little thing, your mind becomes overwhelmed. This is why, when you have a number of problems, get them on paper. Your mind will have a better shot at arriving at ways to take care of them.

I developed a lifetime "to-do" list. I found that I was continually putting off those things since I had no plan to achieve them. After I put these fifty or so items on my list, I committed to doing one per week. Not only am I getting them accomplished, but also I only work on the easiest ones first!

In addition to putting these dreams on paper, I've developed both a vision statement and a mission statement for my life. A vision statement tells you where you're going to be, while a mission statement tells you how you're going to get there.

Along with these statements, I've developed a master list of a number of objectives to focus on for this year. These statements and objectives are looked at daily. The more often you put this information into your head, the easier it is for your mind to help find ways to accomplish them.

Here's another example of how you can use dreams to achieve your results. During the morning while I'm exercising, I play a movie in my mind. This isn't any ordinary movie. This movie is my life exactly as I want it to be. Over the years my movie has changed, as objectives and results have changed in my life. But one thing has remained constant: I have played some kind of movie in my mind every day for the last twenty years.

So what does playing this "mind movie" do for you? For starters, it motivates you to know what you'll be achieving in the future.

Will everything you're seeing happen exactly the way that you want it to by the exact date? Possibly not. But won't life be more fun when you have the self-confidence to achieve many of your objectives?

Writing crystallizes thought, and thought motivates action.
∾ PAUL J. MEYER, SMI, WACO, TX

Action No. 1: On a clean sheet of paper, list as many objectives as you possibly can over the next ten minutes.

Action No. 2: What are all of the little things you've been putting off that just don't seem to get done? On another sheet of paper labeled "My Life To-Do List," begin your "to-do" list right now!

Action No. 3: What's your Vision Statement for your life the way you'd like it to be (this may take awhile, so feel free to come back and answer this question)?

Action No. 4: What's your Mission Statement? In other words how are you going to accomplish your vision?

Action No. 5: What does your movie look like? Begin today to develop a movie of exactly where you'd like to see your life, both personally and professionally. Find a quiet area, lean back, close your eyes, and see your new life. If there's anything that pops up that you're unsure of or would like to change, simply rewind the film and start again.

Once you have this movie exactly the way you want it (and this may take a few days), play it every day at the same time. You'll notice after awhile pieces of your movie may begin to occur.

2) OBJECTIVE FOLDERS

Take charge of your life. You can do with it what you will.

∾ PLATO

As you develop these objectives, it may be necessary to categorize them into various folders. We have so many different things happening in our life and so many various roles we play that it's virtually impossible to remain organized without at least categorizing how, when, and where we'd like everything to happen.

Begin by deciding what life folders you'd like to use. It doesn't matter how many you have (though too many may become unwieldy), what they are called or what category you put an objective into. All that's necessary is that you put these objectives into categories that you want, as long as these categories help you achieve your objectives. These various categories are file folders. You're simply organizing whatever it is you'd like to achieve. It actually doesn't matter which folder you put an objective into. It's just a way to stay organized.

Here are a few category suggestions:

Career
Financial
Ethical
Educational
Health
Social
Cultural
Family
Home

What's important is that you make the decision which categories are important to you. If you pick categories or objectives simply because you feel that you should have them, you're defeating the purpose. Your mind will keep you from achieving your objectives, because you're putting negative information into your head that acts as a brake, while you're also hitting the accelerator. If you were to actually perform this stunt in a car, your vehicle would move forward, but after a while you'd burn out your brakes and destroy your engine.

That's also what would happen to you! Get rid of the guilt you may have about something you think you should or should not do. It's your life; live it as you want, not as somebody else wants. I'm not advocating doing anything illegal, immoral or going against religious beliefs; what I am suggesting is that you can achieve your objectives only if you decide that they are worthwhile.

Carpe Diem.

∽ LATIN: "SEIZE THE DAY."

Action:

a) Take several sheets of paper and write one category on top of each.

b) Take the list of objectives you've written down and decide which of the categories they belong in.

c) Now, prioritize one or two items in each category that are the most important for you to begin focusing on and achieving now.

3) CHART OF ACCOUNTS

*The real measure of your wealth is how much you'd be
worth if you lost all your money.*
∽ AUTHOR UNKNOWN

As a salesperson, not only are you in the business to help your clients achieve their results through the purchase of your products or services, but you also are in the business of earning the income to achieve *your* results.

I've worked with a number of salespeople over the years who would continually complain about not making enough money. First of all, I would ask them how much was enough, and, secondly, I wanted to know how much their current expenses or outflow was. Most couldn't answer either question.

During the lowest period of my life when I felt like I owed money to everybody in the world, I sat down and developed a chart of accounts for myself. This is a list of everybody and every institution you owe money to. Knowing to whom and how much money you owe makes it much easier to earn the money necessary to cover your expenses. As mentioned before, "Writing crystallizes thought and thought motivates action."

Writing down all of your current liabilities acts as a motivator to you and frees your mind to come up with the ways to accomplish your objectives, one of which is having more than enough money to pay your bills.

Now it's just not enough to pay your bills on time. Since you're always going to have some kind of bills to pay each month (utilities, etc.), let's figure out what you currently can get by on (your minimum income) and also what you'd like your standard of living to be (your maximum).

Let's go back to those objectives you've developed. Put dollar figures next to the ones that you'd like to buy. By deciding how much money you'd like to have, you'll be able to develop a plan to get you there. In addition, let's take every item on your income list and decide how much you'd like to be paying each month.

Let's say your rent is now $1000 monthly, but you'd like to purchase a home and you figure that the mortgage would be around $2000. The $1000 rent is your minimum (you can't pay less than that each month), and the $2000 is your current maximum (the amount you'd like to be paying each month, if you were in the home you'd like to be in). Now do this for every item on your account list.

Once you've developed your current and future chart of accounts, the next objective is to shorten your list. It's amazing what you can do when you owe money to very few institutions and can pay cash for everything else. This is truly the feeling of freedom!

Future planning does not deal with anticipation on future needs,
but on the results of present decisions.

∾ AUTHOR UNKNOWN

Action: Begin right now to develop your own chart of accounts. Make a copy of the form that follows to list every account you have (you may want to redo this chart a number of times during your career). But remember, put the bare minimum you can live on in the first column. In addition, go back to your objective folders. Take all of those items you'd like to own, and write in how much you'd like to be paying for them monthly or how much you'd like to be saving in order to pay cash.

Then write down your maximum expenses, the amount you'd like to pay money for to have the lifestyle you want. Someplace between these two totals is what you'd like to be earning. This chart of accounts gives you a vividly clear picture of how and why you'd like to earn the income you have for the yearly maximum total. This may look overwhelming and time-consuming, but it does work. Take your time. There's no need to do this all at once.

		Monthly Minimum	Monthly Maximum
Fixed	Rent or Mortgage	_____	_____
Expenses	Utilities	_____	_____
	Disability Insurance	_____	_____
	Fire/General Insurance	_____	_____
	Income/State Tax	_____	_____
	Property Taxes	_____	_____
	Social Security	_____	_____
	Telephone	_____	_____
	Other	_____	_____
Living	Food	_____	_____
Expenses	Clothing/Footwear	_____	_____

	Laundry/Tailor	_____	_____
	Nonbusiness Meals	_____	_____
	Auto – Nonbusiness	_____	_____
	Doctor/Dentist	_____	_____
	Prescriptions	_____	_____
	Other	_____	_____
Savings	Life Insurance	_____	_____
	Savings Account	_____	_____
	Debt Reduction	_____	_____
	Investments	_____	_____
	Other	_____	_____
Misc.	Tithe/Charities	_____	_____
	Vacation/Entertainment	_____	_____
	Club/Dues	_____	_____
	Gifts/Services	_____	_____
	Other	_____	_____

Total Income Required: _____ _____

X12   X12

Total Income Yearly: _____ _____

(SUCCESS MOTIVATION INSTITUTE, WACO, TX)

4) BUSINESS ACCOUNTS

Money talks . . . but all mine ever says is good-bye.

෭ AUTHOR UNKNOWN

Now, do the same exercise for your business accounts. "But I don't have my own business," you're saying. Whether you're actually in business for yourself or for a large company, you are in your own business and that business is you!

Begin to understand investing in you. This is the key to the entire chapter: How much money do you spend each year on your outside? It's amazing how much money clothes, shoes, makeup, and accessories will cost. But how much are you spending on your inside yearly?

The more money you're putting into yourself (to improve both yourself and your business) the better chance you'll make more money. First of all, any monies you spend to improve yourself and/or to make you a more effective salesperson should be a tax deduction (check with your tax expert on any suggestions made here). The government actually wants to help you to become more successful. In reality, this is one of the few deductions left in the tax code.

Second, any money you spend on yourself should come back to you multiplied. Think of it this way: If I were to offer you a guaranteed return on your investment of a thousand percent, would you take it? Sure you would. But here's what is exciting; you're that investment! You have one of the best assets available to invest in. You have the only investment that you have total control over!

It's easier to adjust ourselves to the hardships of poor living than to adjust ourselves to the hardships of making a better one.

෭ AUTHOR UNKNOWN

Action: Now that you have your personal chart of accounts on paper, begin to list on a copy of the following form all of your expenses, both minimum and maximum. If you had put some business expenses on your personal chart of accounts, you can always take them off and put them on your business side. It's always preferable to keep your personal and business accounts separate, if for no other reason than it helps when filing your income tax.

Another reason to keep these charts separate is to know exactly what it costs to develop and grow your business. You'll see over time that the more you invest in yourself (and thus your business) the larger the return in income.

Once you've totaled both lists, add them together to give yourself a realistic total of why you want to earn that large income. Not only will you know why, but also this will give you a realistic, vivid objective to shoot for!

	Monthly Minimum	Monthly Maximum
Accounting		
Advertising/Contests/Promotion		
Business Note Payments		
Entertainment		
Interest/Bank Charges		
Office Rental/Meeting Rooms		
Personal Development		
Postage		
Printing/Stationery		
Secretarial/Answering Service		
Taxes/Licenses		
Telephone		
Travel/Transportation		
Miscellaneous		
Other		
Total Income Required:		
	X12	X12
Total Business Income:		
	+	+
Total Personal Income:		
(From the last section)		
	=	=
Total Income Objective:		

(SUCCESS MOTIVATION INSTITUTE, WACO, TX)

5) SELF-MANAGEMENT

It's things you can control that make you successful—not that which you can't control.

       ∾ AUTHOR UNKNOWN

Have you ever heard these statements?

"I have no time to see you."

"I wish I could find the time to exercise."

"I'd love to get together with you, but I can't because I have to (fill in the blank)."

"I just can't seem to get it all done."

"I never have enough time to (again, fill in the blank)."

I'll bet you think you hear those statements just from others. In reality, these are also the verbal statements discussed in Part I that we're feeding our minds every day—if not consciously, at least subconsciously.

Why do we feel we have very little time? Is it because we have too much to do? Is it because all the timesaving mechanisms with which we've saturated our lives actually reduce our time available? Or is it because the times are just changing?

The real answer is that any control over time must begin from within. Therefore, time management is not the issue. "Self-management" is where we need to begin. If we can't manage ourselves within the time available, we'll be forever lost in the jungle of control.

Reread the statements at the beginning of this section again. Do you notice each one begins with the first-person pronoun "I?" That means "I" am in control, and when you tell yourself and others that you "can't" do something, you are saying you are either giving up control or you have no control.

The only asset we have is our time. We have twenty-four hours a day to use or lose. We do have total control over what we do in relation to the time available. As a matter of fact, we have an abundance of time, if we choose to believe we do.

So how do we go about being a better time/self manager? Step one is to begin rephrasing what you say. Say:

"I do have time to see you. Let's see where it best fits into our schedules."

"I always have time to exercise. Here's when I'll do it."

"I'd love to get together with you. Let's do it . . ."

"I always get everything accomplished in the time allotted."

"I always accomplish everything I plan."

By rephrasing your verbal statements, your mind begins to cause you to act the way you truly want to.

Step two is to write down everything on a monthly calendar, including those items you used to think you couldn't do, such as exercising. Find a time to do it and stick with it.

Step three is to take one part of your life and commit to making just one change. Never attempt to change more than ten percent of anything at one time. Otherwise, you end up doing nothing at all.

Remember how you eat an elephant: one bite at a time! And tell someone else what you are going to do. The easiest person to break a commitment to is yourself. Once you've asked a friend to check up on you, you're bound to begin the change. And once you've made it, you'll realize how easy it is to make even more changes.

Step four is to make the decision to make that change RIGHT NOW, before you stop reading. Otherwise, you'll continue the insidious habit of procrastination.

On the plains of hesitation, bleached the bones of countless millions, who upon the very brink of success, sat down to wait. And while waiting they withered and died!

∽ AUTHOR UNKNOWN

Action: Begin now to work on the suggested steps:

1) Think of some of the phrases you use to comment about time. Write down five statements that reflect time in not only a positive tone, but also reflecting your abundance of time.

A. _____

_____

B. _____

_____

C. _____

_____

D. _____

_____

E. _____

_____

2) Check your monthly planner/calendar. Is everything you can possibly accomplish written on it? Spend some time today reviewing all your business and personal activities. List as many of these as you can on your calendar for the next twelve months.

3) What part of your life would you like to begin to change the most? Begin to list a few areas so that over the next few weeks you'll have arrived at one specific change that you'd like to begin working on.

A. _____

_____

B. _____

_____

C. _____

_____

D. _____

_____

E. _____

_____

4) Begin working on the previous three steps right now!

6) HIGH-PAYOUT ACTIVITIES

If you play at a high level, the bounces go your way.
∾ TOM LANDRY

As we discussed in the last section, the key to success, the key to achieving your objectives, is to manage yourself first because without self-management you'll never accomplish your results. There's no such thing as "time management." Time pretty well manages itself. It's a matter of managing *yourself.*

Step one is to figure out what your top six high-payout activities are. High-payout activities are the items that you're paid the big bucks for. For instance, if your boss were to pull you aside and ask you what you do that would cause him to keep you employed, what would you tell him? Those are your HPAs (high-payout activities).

Begin with your most important HPAs. What do you do that pays you the most money? That's right, getting "face-to-face" with the customer. This is "seeing the whites of their eyes." Nothing you do has a higher value. If you could just wiggle your nose and only be in front of customers all day, your income would skyrocket.

Priority number two should be setting yourself up to be in front of your prospects and clients. This could be asking for meetings either in person or by telephone (though the phone is always more time productive when you are setting up a number of meetings at one time).

The number three HPA is getting referrals. Nothing in your arsenal of tools can be leveraged as highly as the ability to have names of individuals that have been referred to you by someone they respect and that also have the ability to buy.

From here, you need to develop the rest of your HPAs to focus on. Remember an HPA is something that's done during your business hours. An LPA (low-payout activity) is something that could be done after business hours (i.e., paperwork, contracts, follow-up, etc.). That's not to say that you shouldn't do these activities during business hours, only that your HPAs should take priority.

If we do all that is necessary, all the odds are in our favor.
∾ HENRY KISSINGER

Action No. 1: Write down your top daily high-payout activities. Remember that these are the activities that pay you and your business the highest return. You may want to use the above suggestions for your top three HPAs.

Activity:

A. _____

_____

B. _____

_____

C. _____

_____

D. _____

_____

E. _____

_____

Action No. 2: Decide right now to do your top three HPAs every day and always make them your priority, no matter what else happens.

I focus on accomplishing my top high-payout activities everyday!

7) THE SELF-MANAGEMENT SYSTEM

It's easy to know and do right. When in doubt,
simply do whatever you least like to do.

ᖚ AUTHOR UNKNOWN

Now that you have your HPAs developed, it's time to get the rest of your processes organized.

1) Write down the top five areas that keep you from doing your HPAs. These are low-payout activities (LPAs) and are the items that could be real or simply excuses for not doing what you know you should:
   a) Paperwork (shouldn't be done during your prime hours)
   b) Busy work (activities not directly tied to making money)
   This is not to say that some of these activities are not important. But these activities could be postponed for a time when you can't do your HPAs, such as before 8 A.M. or after 5 P.M.

2) Make a commitment to only focus on the HPAs and refuse to do the LPAs during prime time (LPAs are those items that either make you no money directly or items that can be performed outside of your prime "selling" hours without any repercussions).

3) Understand the difference between "urgent" and "important":
   a) Urgent: activities that demand your immediate attention
   b) Important: has to do with results and objectives

Therefore, activities that are both **urgent** and **important** demand your attention and must be done immediately because they have to do with the results you're attempting to achieve. A crisis is an example of any activity that is both urgent (demands immediate attention) and important (has to do with results).

Activities that are **not urgent** but **important** are the activities that make you the most money. These are the activities that involve planning, thinking and work. These are the activities that aren't fun in the normal sense of the word. Anytime you have to think, it feels like work. And anytime an activity makes you think, you prefer not to do it and you put it off. Here's the difference between successful salespeople and the average salesperson: successful salespeople do what's necessary to make them successful. Unsuccessful salespeople wait for something to happen.

Organization begins with the successful salesperson deciding to accomplish as much as they can in as little time as possible. My father used to say that he was "lazy." What he meant was that he wanted to do as little work as he had to do to become successful. He discovered what had to be done, didn't put it off, but made it happen.

Just do the monotonous execution of the obvious.

∾ AUTHOR UNKNOWN

Action No. 1: What are those low-payout activities that are keeping you from accomplishing your objectives? List the five key LPAs to help you understand what you need to reduce and eliminate from your professional life.

1. _____

_____

2. _____

_____

3. _____

_____

4. _____

_____

5. _____

_____

Action No. 2: Decide to spend one hour each week looking back on what you did last week and planning what you'll be doing next week. When will that be?

_____

8) FOCUS ON THE "IMPORTANT"

Character is the ability to carry out plans made long after the desire has left.
∽ AUTHOR UNKNOWN

As a salesperson, you must focus on what is important (your objectives to achieve) instead of what's urgent (brush fires that occur on a daily basis). We're going to focus on your "important" tasks rather than your "urgent" tasks, because urgent tasks tend to get taken care of without much additional effort.

Because of a lack of objectives, many salespeople are motivated more by what is urgent in their lives than by what is important. Urgent tasks tend to consume you, so that by the end of the day many tasks have been completed, but no movement in any specific direction has occurred.

Individuals can only be motivated by what is important through developing a strong focus on results. Important tasks keep salespeople on track, no matter what is happening, and keep salespeople focused on results rather than on methods.

Too many salespeople are so task-oriented that they keep doing the same things the same way every day, hoping against hope that what they are doing will bring them different and better results. In reality, if they would focus on their objectives —what is important, not what is urgent—they would keep on track, albeit experiencing a little pain, and accomplish enough of the right tasks for success.

Definition of Insanity: Doing the same things over and over while expecting different results!
∽ AUTHOR UNKNOWN

Most salespeople have good intentions about accomplishing as many important items as they can each day. In this context, important refers to objectives and tasks that will move salespeople toward success. But if they are not focused on the important items with a plan and the deadlines and action steps necessary to keep them on track, then what is urgent keeps them going around in circles.

For example, you've planned your day the evening before with all the important items that need to be accomplished tomorrow, including your appointments and objectives. You arise with full anticipation of hitting the ground running on your "to-do" list. But since you haven't made a commitment to your plan and you haven't factored urgent items into the equation, you quickly get off course. (Urgent refers to whatever comes up that needs your immediate attention, such as a customer calling with an emergency or a family crisis.)

If you focus daily on what is urgent, you're spinning in circles without any growth—always fighting fires. Your important tasks become less and less clear, until they fade from memory, with only a slight hope of ever being accomplished.

If your focus is on the important agenda, however, while dealing with whatever is urgent, you will grow as your objectives and plans move you to a higher plateau. You will pull yourself back to what's important after any type of crisis.

Use a planner to keep yourself focused on your important activities. Here are a few useful ideas. Some of these have already been covered, but plan to use what you can now, and add more at a later time:

1) <u>HPAs</u>: Have a checklist of items you have to take care of every day.
2) <u>To-dos</u>: Write down the activities that you want to do every day. Check them off after they are completed.
3) Keep your <u>objectives</u> in your planner and look at them every morning.
4) Keep <u>verbal</u> <u>statements</u> to read and refer to.
5) Keep a list of <u>important numbers</u> (credit card numbers, airline numbers, etc.).
6) Keep a list of <u>bills to pay</u> and when you'll pay them.
7) Keep a complete <u>phone record</u> of all your clients with you.
8) <u>Do it, dump it, delegate it or delay it</u>: Whenever you write an activity down, either do it, dump it and forget about it, delegate it to somebody else or delay it to another day or time. This isn't procrastination since you're making a conscious effort to make sure the activity gets accomplished.
9) Whenever you set an <u>appointment</u>, write in not only the name of your prospect, but also the date you set the appointment (so you know how long ago and when you set it). Also, write down the location. You may be setting a number of appointments, and you don't want to be setting appointments too close together that may be on opposite sides of town.
10) <u>Carry</u> your planner with you at all times.
11) Keep <u>month-at-a-glance calendars</u> to set all important dates, both personal and professional, out into the future.
12) Always prepare your entire day <u>the night before</u>. When you walk into the office the next day, no matter what happens, no matter what crisis may occur, you're set because you set yourself up ahead of time.

13) <u>Commit to your plan</u>: Many salespeople develop a plan but don't stick to it. How many times have you walked into the office in the morning with your plan and had a crisis occur as soon as you walked in? Committed salespeople don't let the crisis throw them off-track. As soon as the crisis is taken care of, they immediately go back to their plan, like a magnet.

(SUCCESS MOTIVATION INSTITUTE, WACO, TX)

Things that matter most must never be at the mercy of things that matter least.

∾ JOHANN WOLFGANG VON GOETHE

The process to focus on what's "important" is to develop a weekly planning guide. At first glance, a weekly planning guide looks like nothing more than a time planner. This is far from reality. Though the weekly planning guide could be used as a planner, its number one use is that as a visualization of the future.

Since our mind is like a magnet, attracting that which we are focusing on requires deciding exactly what you want your business to look like. On the weekly planning guide, plan out exactly what you want your "ideal week" to look like. Write in:

a) When you'd like to be face-to-face in front of prospects (based on the number you'd like to be achieving). Preferably the same time daily
b) When you'd like to be on the phone contacting prospects (same time every day)
c) Any sales meetings you have on a weekly basis (this way you'll never schedule an appointment when you shouldn't)
d) Travel time
e) . . . Etc.

When you've developed your weekly planning guide, you now can begin to attract the activities you want to perform. Most individuals are very poor time planners. By having a weekly planning guide and knowing what you want to be doing at any given time, you can plan exactly when you want to see prospects by just filling in the blanks on your guide. This way, your week is based on what you want, not what someone else wants. (We'll be discussing more about this in Part Three—The Contact.)

What we do before 9, after 5 and on Saturdays determines how well we do in life.

∾ TY BOYD

Action No. 1: Begin using a planner and develop some of the suggested steps above.

Action No. 2: Make a copy of the form below and fill in your "ideal" sales week.

	Monday	**Tuesday**	**Wednesday**	**Thursday**	**Friday**	**Saturday**
7:00						
7:30						
8:00						
8:30						
9:00						
9:30						
10:00						
10:30						
11:00						
11:30						
12:00						
12:30						
1:00						
1:30						
2:00						
2:30						
3:00						
3:30						
4:00						
4:30						
5:00						
5:30						
6:00						

9) DAILY SALES ACTIVITIES

The will to win is worth nothing unless you have the will to prepare.

∾ AUTHOR UNKNOWN

Now that you've developed your top six HPAs, let's break down your sales activities from yearly all the way down to daily activity, including a "success target" that tells you exactly what you must do to achieve your objectives.

First of all, begin by deciding your yearly objective. This objective can be your yearly income, number of sales or possibly even the total gross volume you'd like to sell this year. This can be the figure you've arrived at as you developed your chart of accounts and business accounts. Next, for each of the high-payout activities you developed earlier, put a number down for how much of each activity you'll need to accomplish for the year.

Continue through this procedure by dividing your yearly figures by twelve to give you a monthly number; divide the yearly number by fifty (hopefully, you'll be taking two weeks off for vacation) to get your weekly figure; and finally divide your weekly figure by five to arrive at a daily figure for activity. This number is your magic activity number ... your success target. Once you arrive at this figure, all you'll need to do is to accomplish this activity daily without thinking. No matter what happens during the day, no matter how many crises attempt to get you off-track, you accomplish your daily objective.

Many salespeople want to beat this system and take shortcuts in their activity. They don't believe they need to perform this level of activity to become successful. As a result, many salespeople become creative and design the activity level they want to do, not the activity level that is needed to become successful.

The activity level you develop now is the activity habit you'll continue for a lifetime. Is it too late to increase your activity habit? No, but you must concentrate and focus on your objectives to break through your current lack of activity. Now you have a reason for achieving the results and activity you want.

Remove those activities that are not moving you toward the achievement of your objectives. Ask yourself, "Is what I'm doing moving me to where I want to be?"

Spare me your intelligence for six months and do what I tell you to do.
∾ PAUL J. MEYER

Action: Refer to Part One – "Results" and transfer your answers to this Action Step. Your "Success Target" is the amount of activity you must accomplish in each category to make one sale. You may not know this number now, but after keeping track of your activity numbers for the next three weeks, you should have a pretty good working number for what it takes to hit your "success target." (More about this in the next section.)

Activity	(Objective) #Yearly	#Monthly	#Weekly	#Daily	Success Target
1.					
2.					
3.					
4.					
5.					
6.					
7.					
8.					
9.					
10.					

10) SUCCESS TARGET

A number watched does what you want it to.

∽ AUTHOR UNKNOWN

How do you arrive at your "success target?" Simply figure out what it takes to make one sale. For example, let's say you made ten sales this month. Divide every activity category by ten to tell you, on average, what it takes to make one sale. This figure should help you develop your weekly activity levels based on what it will take you to make that one sale. This is simple. Just do the activity necessary to make the sale.

By working with your activity this way, the amount of activity it takes to make your sales will diminish. Keep your activity level at the same pace, and your sales will skyrocket!

As we discussed in the last section, your "success target" is designed to help you understand not only what it takes to make one sale, but also what level of activity must be accomplished to reach your objectives. If you increase your sales objectives, you simply increase the level of activity correspondingly.

For instance, let's say your current daily activity level to make one sale is the following:

	20	Referrals
	15	Contacts
	5	Appointments
	4	Presentations
	3	Negotiation Interviews
=	1	Sale

All that's necessary to increase your sales objectives is to increase your activity level. Let's say you want a 25 percent increase. Your new daily activity level would look like this:

	25	Referrals
	19	Contacts
	6	Appointments
	5	Presentations
	4	Closing Interviews
=	1.25	Sales

All you now need to do is simply, without thinking, accomplish your daily activity level. In the next section, we'll discuss how to focus on your daily activity.

Successful people are influenced by the desire for pleasing results.
Failures are influenced by the desire for pleasing methods and are satisfied
with results from doing things they like to do.

∾ ALBERT E.N. GRAY

Action: Answer the following questions to understand your "success target," and add your answers to the chart from the last section.

1. What do I have to do daily to achieve my objective?

_____

2. Based on my current level of activity, what will it take to make one sale?

_____

3. Divide my sales activities for the last three weeks into the number of sales I've made.

_____

4. The number I receive for each activity is the number it takes to achieve one sale.

_____

11) CORRECT, CONSISTENT DAILY ACTIVITY—SCOREKEEPING

Thought determines what you want. Action determines what you'll get.
∾ AUTHOR UNKNOWN

Now that you know what your activity level needs to be, make sure you have a game plan. You do this with "correct, consistent, daily activity!"

Most salespeople have CDA, Consistent Daily Activity, but it isn't necessarily correct daily activity. I was included in this group and, as a result, I wasn't achieving many objectives. During a self-analysis session, I also realized:

a) I didn't have "correct" activity.

b) I enjoyed playing more than I enjoyed working.

c) Playing wouldn't pay the bills and wouldn't pay for the play.

I also realized I enjoyed playing games and being involved in sports. All sports involve numbers and scores. Sports are also fun. So I decided to take the best parts of playing and add them to the work mix of tracking to at least make working fun.

I came up with a tool to make sure that I was having fun with my work and that I was tracking my activity to give me the results I wanted. The result was "correct, consistent daily activity" or the CCDA checklist.

If you can measure it, you can manage it!
∾ AUTHOR UNKNOWN

Keep score of your daily activities and reward yourself based on your correct, consistent daily activity (CCDA), rather than only on your results.

Play the game and control your own results by controlling your activity. In every professional and amateur sport, athletes keep score. Salespeople generally have no idea how to develop a daily plan to organize their sales activity. To help you do this, use an activity checklist.

Salespeople need a tracking system for the high activity level required to create sales. This system is based on the 80/20 formula (Pareto's Law): 80 percent of the things you do are accomplished in 20 percent of the time. If you can isolate those activities that are most important and spend more time doing them, you will accomplish more and realize a higher payout (these are your HPAs that you've developed).

Begin by giving each of the tracking activities a point value. I made sure that the activity, which was the farthest from the sale, received the fewest points. The closest activity received the most points. Also, I made sure that the activities I had the most control over also had the fewest points. I then decided on the daily activity objective. You'll notice in the example that the objective is twice what a sale is worth. I realized that if a sale were equal to the daily point objective, whenever I made my sale, I'd quit for the day.

I then developed an objective for a bonus day. By achieving this level, I allowed myself to buy something. Or if there was something I really wanted, I had to achieve my bonus total before I could have it. Let's say I wanted new clothes. Before I could buy anything, I had to hit my bonus. That was the incentive (more about the bonus later).

The CCDA checklist prioritizes and applies a point system to the high-payout activities that need to be accomplished on a regular basis. Here's an example of how a checklist might look:

Sale	100	points
Close	50	points
Presentation	25	points
Appointment	10	points
Referral	5	points
Contact	1	point
Total:	200	points/day
Bonus:	300	points

In this example, the daily commitment for the salesperson is to reach 200 points. Salespeople need to make an absolute commitment to achieving their objective daily.

Winners keep track of results; losers keep track of reasons!
❧ AUTHOR UNKNOWN

But the focus is on activity, which is controllable, rather than on sales (results) which are not. When the focus in on the correct activity necessary to reach the sales objectives, then your mind is directed toward what is important and necessary to achieve the results, rather than just on results.

My daily result statement was:

I only go home when my objective has been achieved.

The objective was 200 points, and I had to achieve these points in any way possible.

Again, the CCDA checklist apportions fewer points to those activities that you have less control over. Thus, to achieve the daily objective, you must maintain high activity in the areas over which you have control.

For example: Let's say that today I have no sales and no closes. I made three presentations for seventy-five points. I made five appointments for fifty points, received five referrals for twenty-five points, and made ten contacts for ten points. By 5 P.M. I had a total of 160 points. What do I do now?

Now we go back to controlling the controllable. Remember that I made the commitment to achieve my objective of 200 points every day no matter what. So I now need to get the additional forty points by doing the activities I have control over: contacts, referrals and appointments. By getting on the phone and making calls, I can get my forty points in any number of combinations.

This is the "Law of Delayed Return." By working your activity correctly and doing what's controllable, sooner or later the correct activity leads to a sale.

CCDA also works when you pursue your activity focused on the results you want to attain. This is the "Law of Averages." This law requires patience. It can't be forced or hurried. But if you do the activity necessary, the result will be there; we just can't predict exactly when.

A number of years ago, a nine-year-old girl set a record selling Girl Scout cookies. As a matter of fact, she sold so many, Disney made a movie about her called "The Cookie Kid." Here's how she focused on her CCDA:

I do my homework, then I go around to the lobbies about 5:00. I work until 8:00 or 8:30, and practically all day on Saturdays, from 10:00 until 8:00 P.M. Once you start, you have to stick with it.

This young lady focused on the correct, consistent daily activity. By understanding what it took to become successful, she simply did the activity necessary, and the results took care of themselves.

Most salespeople consider the day a success only when a sale is made. In many sales careers, a daily sale is not a normal occurrence; or, if it is, the salesperson considers the day a failure if there isn't a sale. More people don't buy from salespeople than do, so by focusing on daily activity, you will achieve and have control over the intended results.

For the highly motivated salesperson, add the "bonus day" to the CCDA. When you hit your bonus points, reward yourself from your "want" list. Catalogs are a great list source for these "wants." You should write down what you want in the $25 to $100 price range. These items are generally items you want but don't need—in other words, items that can motivate. This idea also helps solidify commitment toward an objective. When there is something of value that you want this week, the bonus serves as the target and motivation for achieving it.

As we discussed earlier, it's all right to set an objective and do everything you can to achieve it, yet possibly just miss. It's also all right to achieve the objective by working on the activity and accomplishing it. But it's not all right to set an objective and passively work toward it. That's setting up the habits of failure. So make sure you do not go home until your activity objective for the day is achieved.

Tracking sales activity with a point system provides feedback to the salesperson. Feedback corrects your course toward your objectives. To help improve your performance, increase your feedback. The more you work on where you've been, the more effective you're going to be in increasing your results. Realize that this is a self-competition. You can't compete with somebody else because you can't control others. You only have control over yourself.

Keep track of your best days, best weeks and best months in all activity categories. Remember,

---

A number watched does whatever you want it to do.
ॐ AUTHOR UNKNOWN

If you want to improve your closing (negotiation) skills, track your negotiation average and ask 10,000 people to buy. Whatever you track and focus on will improve. If you know where you are at all times, you'll become more effective. You have to know where you are starting from to get to where you want to go.

When the focus is on the activity necessary to reach your sales objective, then your mind is focused on what's important and necessary to achieve the results, rather than on the results themselves, while neglecting the correct activity.

Winners are prepared and prepared ahead of time. Winners have a positive expectancy to win. They believe in advance that they are going to make it happen. Winners are specific and positive about their winning. They accept personal responsibility for their actions. "It's my fault and no one else's!" They pay the price willingly because they know it's a bargain. Winners set objectives and achieve them.

Its not the conditions that gets the results—it's the system.

ᓚ AUTHOR UNKNOWN

Action No. 1: On your pad of paper, develop your CCDA checklist by writing down those HPAs you developed earlier and attaching a point value to them. Remember that the further an activity is from making a sale, such as a phone call, the lower the amount of points you may want to give to it.

As you are developing your daily objective total, make the number a stretch so that it takes some effort to make it happen. Notice in the example that my objective was 200 points daily, yet a sale was 100. As mentioned, this was because I knew that if the daily objective was 100 points, I would quit for the day whenever I made a sale.

Take your time developing your checklist. You may need to play with it for a few weeks until you have it to your liking. It took me a few weeks of tweaking to get it "just right!"

Activity   **Points**

1. _____

_____

2. _____

_____

3. _____

_____

4. _____

_____

5. _____

_____

6. _____

_____

7. _____

_____

8. _____

_____

9. _____

_____

10. _____

_____

Daily Objective: _____
This is the number you live and sell by.

This is your verbal statement:

_____

I go home only when my objective has been achieved!

Action No. 2: One of the major reasons any professional salesperson makes large amounts of money is because of their ability to develop a tracking method for all of their activity. We discussed CCDA. Now is your chance to put it to work.

On a spreadsheet, put the working days of the week along the left side. Along the top put all the activities you normally do in a day to make a sale. (See the following Actions.)

The total will be on the bottom. But the most important item across the top is the results you will be forecasting. This way you can make sure you're accomplishing your activity on a daily basis. There's no thinking involved, just doing. Your thought process can now focus on how to make the sale, not where the activity is going to come from.

On a daily basis, simply put a hash mark next to each of the activities as you accomplish them. Should you carry this sheet with you? Absolutely, a pen has a longer memory than your mind.

But isn't this tedious and boring? Sure it can be, but let's put some fun into it.

Make a copy of the form below, or redo one for yourself with the activities you'd like to track. Note that "points" refers to your CCDA checklist, "ST" refers to your success target and "objective" is the activity number you'd like to achieve this week, which could be the same as the checklist and your success target.

Now, simply keep track of your daily activity. Once you've tracked your activity for three weeks, develop your success target. Your success target simply tells you on a moment-to-moment basis exactly what you have to do to make one sale.

Do this on a daily basis forever and your income will continue to increase forever!

Week: Activity:	(1) Contacts	(2) Appts	(3) Pres	(4) Negotiations	(5) Sales	(6) Leads	(7) $s	(8) #s
Points:								
ST:								
Objective:								
Monday:								
Tuesday:								
Wednesday:								
Thursday:								
Friday:								
Saturday:								
Total:								
Total Points:								

(SUCCESS MOTIVATION INSTITUTE, WACO, TX)

Action No. 3: What good is keeping track of your activity without knowing what it means? Every week, when you're adding up all of your hash marks on your tracking report, spend a little time figuring out exactly what the value of your activity was.

When you know the ratios and how each activity compares to the next, you have much more control over your selling activities than 95 percent of the other salespeople out in the marketplace. First of all, most salespeople never keep track of their activity. And, second, very few keep track of their ratios.

I ask salespeople what their negotiation (closing) average is. "I don't know," or "somewhere around ..." generally tends to be the answers I receive. Don't get into the trap of thinking you know where you are without tracking. This is like the ostrich with his head in the ground. Just because you can't see it, doesn't mean it doesn't exist.

The tracking report and ratios are two of the major tools to keep sharp and ready from your sales toolbox. Keeping track this way is the equivalent of an accountant keeping track of how the money is earned and spent. Imagine a business running without any kind of financial tracking.

As you are figuring your ratios, compare this week to last week and this month to last month. Two pieces of information come out of this. First, you can see how well you're improving over time. And second, should you have a slow period, you can quickly see where the improvements need to be made and adjust the activities accordingly.

Develop a spreadsheet to answer the following questions (remember that this can all be put on a computer spreadsheet to make the calculations much easier).

The numbers after the column refer to the column numbers on the previous tracking report.

What is the Objective?

	This Week	Last Week	This Month	Last Month
1) Total Commission Earned:				
2) Negotiation Average (Column 5/4):				
3) Earning per Presentation:				
4) Contacts to Appointments (2/1):				
5) Appointments to Sales (Column 5/2):				
6) Cancellation Ratio (Column 2/3):				
7) Sales to Presentations (Column 5/3):				
8) Contacts to Sales (Column 5/1):				
9) $ Value of Each Contact (Commissions/1):				

(SUCCESS MOTIVATION INSTITUTE, WACO, TX)

12) SUCCESS CHECKLIST

Eighty percent of success is showing up.

∾ WOODY ALLEN

When I was fifteen years old, a friend's older brother was a private pilot and had a small plane. Against the advice from my parents, I went up for a ride. I was hooked! After college, I took flying lessons and received my private pilot's license.

During my ground school training, I learned some very good advice that I hadn't realized would apply to the sales profession until years later. The first thing any pilot does before attempting to take off is to go over the preflight checklist. This is usually a laminated card that sits in the side pocket, which lists every item to go over prior to flying. It became clear that this procedure is the most important task that a pilot performs.

Years later, I realized the same is true for the sales profession. The "success checklist" was designed to keep you on track on a weekly basis. During a period when I had a number of salespeople working with me, I had them fill out this checklist on a weekly basis, and we would track the number of "yes" actions that would be checked off. This would serve as a way to motivate the salespeople to increase the number of correct, consistent, daily activities that must be performed on a regular basis.

The "Success Checklist" has seven main areas to focus on during the week:

Objectives
Prospects
Contacts
Presentations
Self-Management
Attitude
Product Knowledge

Each of these areas has questions to ask yourself to see if you've actually completed the activity, as you said you would. Not only does the checklist serve as a reminder of what to do each week, but it also keeps you honest in terms of what you are and are not doing.

The sheet also has blank spaces to fill in so that you can customize your checklist to fit the objectives you are attempting to achieve. Along with the ratios form that you were introduced to, the "success checklist" serves as a magnet to keep you reminded of the "correct consistent daily activity" that you must do to achieve the results you're shooting for.

In this world, we either discipline ourselves, or we are disciplined by the world.
I prefer to discipline myself.

∾ DICK CAMPBELL

Action: Make copies of the success checklist below. Each week, fill in the blank spaces and keep track of how many "yes" actions you've accomplished the prior week. By using the checklist, you'll begin to see yourself developing the correct habits necessary for achieving great results! (Prospects, contacts and presentations will be dealt with in detail in Part Three.)

I) Objectives

Yes   *No*

1) Weekly income objective of $ _____   _____ _____
2) Weekly sales objective of $ _____   _____ _____

II) Prospects

1) _____ new prospects daily   _____ _____
2) _____ referrals after each sale   _____ _____
3) Adequate information on each referral   _____ _____
4) Used three prospecting methods daily   _____ _____
5) Used the prospect system daily   _____ _____

III) Contacts

1) Called at same place and time daily   _____ _____
2) Prepared _____ prospect cards before phone time   _____ _____
3) Used a planned telephone approach   _____ _____
4) Used the CCDA tracking report   _____ _____
5) Contacted _____ new prospects daily   _____ _____
6) Made at least _____ new appointments daily   _____ _____

IV) Presentations

    1) Planned each presentation   _____ _____

    2) Completed each presentation in allotted time _____ _____

    3) Reassured with confidence   _____ _____

    4) Met negotiation objective of _____%   _____ _____

    5) Genuinely interested in client's needs   _____ _____

    6) Good listener   _____ _____

V) Self-Management

    1) Used weekly plan sheet daily   _____ _____

    2) Scheduled appointments geographically   _____ _____

    3) Know how much an hour is worth   _____ _____

    4) Used to-do list daily   _____ _____

VI) Attitude

    1) Used verbal statements and visualization daily _____ _____

    2) Worked on improving one specific selling skill _____ _____

    3) Positive mental attitude toward business   _____ _____

    4) Have I "seen the whites of their eyes?"   _____ _____

VII) Product Knowledge

    1) Adequate, detailed product knowledge   _____ _____

    2) Spend 15 minutes/day learning   _____ _____

(SUCCESS MOTIVATION INSTITUTE, WACO, TX)

13) MRO CHART

The Lord gives us everything at the price of effort.
∾ LEONARDO DA VINCI

Salespeople work hard for twelve months to reach their yearly objective and then relax during the holidays. When they report back to work in January, they now have a new objective to hopefully get excited about, but their sense of "motivation" is diminished. This is because the new objective is sooooooo far away!

Since it's hard to get excited about an objective twelve months into the future, some other type of trigger or objective needs to be put into place to help salespeople get energized to work as hard if not harder toward their objective.

The tool to do this, and also another way to track your results is with the MRO chart. MRO stands for:

Minimum

Realistic

Optimistic

Here you have a chance to track yourself, based on three different objectives. Your Minimum result is the number you give to your manager. This is also your do or die projection. You hit it no matter what. The reason you give it to your boss is because you're probably going to go above it. Then, you'll look like a hero. Remember the customer service axiom: underpromise and overperform. Your boss is also your customer.

Your Realistic projection is the number you'd really like to hit. This is the one you are preparing and striving for. You're bound to arrive at least somewhere between your minimum projection and your realistic objective. The Optimistic number is the one that is a dream right now, that eventually you'll hit, but you could hit it this month if everything happened exactly the way you want it to. We're not betting on this one yet.

This is a tracking procedure that allows you to see at a glance where you are on a daily basis. Get yourself a piece of graph paper (see "action" illustration that follows). Make two lines. The horizontal line on the bottom would be your time line, days, months, weeks, quarters or years. The vertical line attached over the horizontal line on the right would be your number of units or dollars.

Let's assume you're developing your chart to track your monthly sales beginning in January. Along the bottom of the chart you'd write in the working days of the month, anywhere from twenty-one to thirty-one, depending on the numbers of actual selling days you have based on your business. Along the right-hand side, put the number of units you'd like to sell this month or the dollar volumes.

Now, simply circle your MRO—minimum, realistic and optimistic objectives—on the vertical line. Run three straightedge lines from the bottom left-hand side of your graph where the first day begins, to your three projections.

On a daily basis, simply fill in a box on the day you made a sale or added dollars to your month. You now can see visually where you are toward achieving any of your three projections on a daily basis.

The secret of success is constancy of purpose.

∾ BENJAMIN FRANKLIN

Action: Get graph paper and duplicate the MRO chart below to fit the objectives you're shooting for. Simply put your time line on the bottom, and along the right-hand side put the number of units or dollars you'd like to track over that time period.

Next, circle your minimum, realistic and optimistic objectives. Using a straight edge, draw a line from the bottom left-hand corner to each objective. Then, as you make a sale, simply fill in the space on the graph that corresponds to what you've sold. On a moment-to-moment basis, you'll have more motivation knowing exactly where you are in relation to each of your objectives.

MRO (Minimum/Realistic/Optimistic)

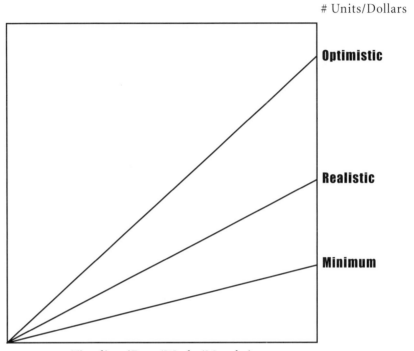

Sell When You See the Whites of Their Eyes!

PART THREE:

The Nine-Step Sales Process

If nobody sells, a terrible thing happens . . . nothing!

∾ AUTHOR UNKNOWN

Once you begin to put the plan you developed from Part II – Tracking Steps to Success! into effect, selling becomes a very basic process, and you most always achieve your objectives. You rarely, if ever, have bad weeks; and if you do, by tracking your results, you simply increase your activity level to get back on track.

There are only two ways to make more money. Sell more of what you sell to more people or sell more of what you sell to the same people. The latter is much easier. Why? Because these individuals have already done business with you, and you've developed their trust . . . they've pulled down their "garbage can lid" and you can "see the whites of their eyes!"

Before we begin, though, there are a few rules to keep in mind as you begin working with your prospect:

a) **Get focused:** Your role in working with your prospect is to sell not your product or service, but to sell yourself by finding out what it is your prospect really wants.

b) **Believe:** Believe in your product/service, believe in your profession, and most importantly, believe in yourself.

c) **Develop a trust relationship:** You need to spend as much time as it takes to understand your prospect's wants so you can develop the solutions together. The quality of this relationship determines the quality of your success.

d) **Make sure your prospect is involved throughout the process:** This is a team effort. The trust relationship begins here.

e) **Selling is education:** Make yourself a consultant to your prospect. Help your prospect learn as much new information as they can to help you help them.

f) **Your profession is your mission:** When your prospect feels and understands your passion, they'll buy for life.

g) **Under promise and over deliver:** This is the easiest way to exceed your prospect's expectations.

h) **Do whatever it takes:** Most salespeople fall short, so go the extra mile.

i) **Give service before selling:** As a salesperson, you're in the service business. The more you do for the prospect, the more they'll do for you . . . they'll buy!

j) **Have fun:** Don't take your business and yourself too seriously. Be serious about your commitment, but enjoy the process and the journey.

It's not what you see . . . it's what they buy.

☙ AUTHOR UNKNOWN

Action: Which of the above rules will you focus on this week? Write down which one and how you'll use it this week:

Rule: _____

_____

Plan for this week: _____

_____

PROCESS

What you do speaks so loudly that I cannot hear what you say.
ɷ RALPH WALDO EMERSON

Every sales profession involves process steps which, when identified as the correct procedure to make sales, must be followed consistently and blindly. Process Steps are the steps to the sale, from the initial meeting and/or greeting of your prospect to the sale, delivery and follow-up of your client.

These sales process steps should be performed over and over without stopping. Imagine a Ferris wheel. Each car on the Ferris wheel is a step in this nine-step process beginning with referrals. By never getting off of the Ferris wheel, you continue to receive referrals and your repeat business improves.

Here's the suggested "Nine-Step Sales Process:"
1) The Contact–Setting the Meeting
2) The Meeting
3) The Interview–Finding the "Gap"
4) The Presentation–Closing the "Gap"
5) The Negotiation
6) The Reassurance–Handling Objections
7) The Delivery
8) The New Prospect–Getting Referrals
9) The Follow-Up–Relationship Management

This sales process generally begins when you receive the name of a potential client. Next, you begin the first (1) Contact step, which, in most outside sales professions, is the meeting. The next step is the first (2) Meeting where you begin to get to know your prospect. Once you begin to discuss what your prospects want and need, you begin the qualifying step or (3) Interview, where you discover the "Gap." This is the stage where you spend time with your prospect to determine whether you should proceed further. This is also one of your most important steps where the amount of time you spend with your prospective client is crucial.

After you qualify your prospect (which should be your most in-depth step of the process; in many sales professions, this takes more than one visit) you next move to the (4) Presentation step. Here, you'll take the information from the qualifying step and present your product or service based on what your prospect told you they want.

Now that you've discovered that your prospect qualifies and is interested in your product or service, you begin the (5) Negotiation. It's not a "close," because once you get to this point (assuming you've not run any red lights . . . see "Prospect Agreement" below), it's only a matter of understanding "how" your prospect will buy.

Your prospect may object (which is only asking for (6) Reassurance) then once your sale is complete you (7) Deliver your product or service. (8) Referrals are the natural conclusion to your sales presentation. One of the most important steps before your process comes full circle is the (9) Follow-up step or "Relationship Management" with your new client.

These are your Nine Sales Process Steps. If any are skipped or ignored, disaster occurs. In this case, a "disaster" is your prospect not buying after you went to all the effort to develop your referral. There are many sales careers in which the salesperson spends less time in certain areas or may not include certain steps. Throughout this section, we'll see why every step is important, regardless of what type of selling you do. Highly paid professional salespeople in all sales professions practice a selling process similar to the one we're about to unfold.

The key is commitment. Once you're committed, it's hard to back down.
So go ahead and do it, and grow that much stronger and surer.
ꙮ "DAS ENERGI" BY PAUL WILLIAMS

Action: Do you have a strong sales process? If not, make a commitment to begin to use the nine-step sales process outlined. If you do have a process, make a commitment to use it and strengthen it with the suggestions to follow.

"I commit to: _____."

PROSPECT AGREEMENT

Always think in terms of what the other person wants.

∾ JAMES VAN FLEET

The entire nine-step sales process is a series of stoplights. Each of these stoplights is a chance to develop trust with your prospect. In the real world, if you run stoplights long enough, you'll either have an accident or get a ticket. In the sales world, your prospect won't trust you and/or won't buy from you. Either one can be devastating.

To make sure that you and your prospect are comfortable and the "garbage can lid" begins to come down, use this three-step procedure, but think of it as a "three-legged stool."

A colleague of mine, Ben Bellus, taught me this sales analogy. Imagine a three-legged stool. Now cut off one of the legs. Pretty wobbly, isn't it? Sitting on it for any length of time might become very uncomfortable, if not impossible.

So it goes for the prospect agreement. Each of the following three steps is a leg of the stool. Without one of the legs, the agreement (stool) will fail and the customer won't buy. To achieve trust and to ensure that you have the prospect's attention and interest throughout the entire sales process, the prospect agreement is the tool to keep you on track. The three-step prospect agreement consists of the following:

1) Set expectations
2) Do what you say you will do
3) Gain agreement

It's as easy as "1, 2, 3!"

Step one is to "Set expectations" for what will be happening in this step of the sales presentation. "Set expectations" means to prepare the prospect. As a speaker, I was taught to:

    a) Tell the audience what I was going to tell them

    b) Tell them

    c) Tell them what I told them

This is essentially what the prospect agreement is all about.

a) First you tell your prospect what's about to happen

b) Next, you tell or ask your prospect about specific information or questions

c) And finally, you and your prospect agree on what was covered

Step two is to "Do what you say you will do" in order to know and/or to find out what your prospect wants.

Step three is to "Gain agreement" with your prospect so that both of you understand each other as it pertains to the information just exchanged.

By using this three-step procedure, any feeling of "high-pressure" selling will go out the window. Prospects who feel "high-pressure" begin to back off immediately. There's no feeling of trust or confidence. But by using the prospect agreement, you move at the pace of your prospect and allow "low-pressure" techniques to take hold. Anytime a buyer and seller meet, pressure occurs. Your prospect is now putting "pressure" on themselves and only as much as they want to handle.

Let's take each prospect agreement step individually to see how to help your prospect drop their "shield" so that you begin to "see the whites of their eyes!"

"Set expectations"

Prospects want to know what's going to happen next without any surprises. "Setting expectations" is letting the prospect know what to expect. For example, after meeting your prospect, you might "set expectations" by saying, "What I'd like to do for the next few minutes is to ask a few questions about what you might be looking for as it relates to this product or service. May I take a few minutes and take notes while we talk?"

A number of things have happened here. Not only have you prepared your prospect for what will happen next, but you also have been polite about asking if they had the time to give you. In addition, there are no surprises since you asked permission to take notes and you relaxed your prospect by letting them know what will happen next.

A similar situation happens when you visit your dentist. Since you trust your dentist, you willingly agree to any procedure that the dentist suggests.

Before the dentist begins any procedure, he/she lets you know exactly what's going to happen before it actually does. "You're going to feel a little sting as I shoot your gums with the novocaine. Your gums will begin to feel numb and at that time

I'll begin to drill. If at any time you begin to feel any pain, please let me know, and I'll administer additional novocaine!"

Again, a number of things are happening in a short period of time. Your dentist is preparing you for what will happen next. You feel comfortable with your dentist because there are no surprises along the way.

Actually, most professionals do much the same thing. A lawyer prepares the client prior to trial, letting the client know exactly what will happen. A surgeon sits with the patient and calmly tells the patient every step of the procedure.

Your prospects don't like to be surprised. As a matter of fact, the more you tell your prospect what steps will be taken and what will happen next, the more relaxed they will feel with you, the more they will trust you, and you will begin to "see the whites of their eyes!"

"Do what you say you will do"

Now that you've set up your client by helping them understand what is coming next, you must "do what you say you will do" in order to gain agreement.

Presenting is simply giving the prospect whatever information you promised you would give in the "set expectations" stage. This is where you are completing your promise. This is where you do what you say you are going to do. But you need to involve the prospect.

If you are giving information, continue to ask questions and keep the prospect involved. If this is the step where you do nothing but ask questions, ask them in such a way as to make the prospect have additional confidence in you. Many times you can give more information by asking thought-provoking questions.

"Gain agreement"

The final step is to remind the prospect what happened by reviewing benefits and/or summarizing what has just transpired. To "gain agreement" is also asking the prospect to buy. Remember those stoplights we discussed earlier? Here's where you need permission to proceed to the next step. This is where the prospect agrees to what has happened in this step and possibly in previous steps.

This is accomplished by summarizing what your prospect told you. You can do this with bullets, while ending your statement with, "Would you agree?" If your prospect doesn't agree with you, you can always back up and find out what you didn't understand. This doesn't upset your prospect because you are using your communication skills to understand this person, since your prospect wants you to understand them.

What you have accomplished is to "gain agreement" on where the prospect's interest is, and they have granted you implied permission to move on to the next step. You will now move to your next process step and begin the "prospect agreement" process all over again.

By telling your prospect what you're going to tell them and checking for understanding, you'll develop a relationship with your prospect and make more sales with higher commissions.

(NISSAN NORTH AMERICA, GARDENA, CA)

Judge a man by his questions rather than his answers.

∾ VOLTAIRE

Action: Using the procedure outlines, write out your own "prospect agreement" for one of the nine steps:

Step: _____

1. Set expectations: Explain what you're going to do and why

_____

2. Do what you say you're going to do

_____

3. Gain agreement: Transition to the next step

_____

PROCESS STEP NO. 1: THE CONTACT – SETTING THE MEETING

Our doubts are traitors and make us lose the good
we oft might win by fearing to attempt.
∾ WILLIAM SHAKESPEARE

You're holding the name of a new referral in your hands. Now what? It's time to pick up the phone and begin calling. Isn't it interesting how much weight a phone gains over night? The hardest part of making calls is making that first call of the day.

Why have we developed such an aversion to making calls to individuals that we don't know? Part of the answer may be that we don't like rejection. The other part of the answer may have to do with our upbringing.

Did you ever hear your parents say, "Don't talk to strangers"? This is, and will always be, a good suggestion to give to a young child. The problem with this is that no one told you to change once you became a salesperson. What do you now do for a living? You talk to strangers! Isn't it interesting that what you now do for a living is what your parents told you not to do as a child!

So here are a few suggestions to deal with this situation:
1) Tape your hand to the receiver using duct tape. This way you can't put the phone down for long (hopefully this will be a technique you'll never have to use).
2) Make your first call of the day to someone who makes you feel good (i.e., a good client, a friend, your mother or possibly time and temperature)! The key here is that once you make the first call, momentum takes over and you keep going.
3) Decide whom you'll be calling the night before or early in the day before beginning your calls. This way, as soon as you've completed one call, there's no need to fumble with whom to call next, the next name is right in front of you and you keep calling (this works well with technique number one).
4) Have an objective for the number of calls, contacts and meetings/presentations you want to make daily and then hit your objective every day! (See Part Two–10, Success Target)
5) Make your calls from the same place at exactly the same time daily.
6) Have your calls lined up in front of you so that you don't have to put the telephone receiver down after making each call.

7) Read a few telephone statements to yourself prior to making your calls. If you develop the proper attitude, calling becomes much easier. For example, "Everyone I call wants to do business with me!"

A client may give you names that aren't technically referrals (more about this later). They are actually introductions, and that's how you need to treat them. Your first job is to develop a script similar to a negotiation script (again, more about this in the "negotiation" section), except this one you can read to your prospect since you're on the phone.

Low-key plays better than high-pressure, since you want to use the influence of your client to its best advantage. Begin your call with a short statement and a question. For instance, "John, this is Sam Stone with ABC Technologies. We haven't met, but Jim Smith asked me to give you a call. Do you have a moment?" This is the beginning of your prospect agreement.

Asking this question is important because a call is always an intrusion on your prospect's time. You've also positioned yourself since you mentioned the name of the individual who has influence over your prospect. You're now in control because you asked a question. Now, your prospect will have to answer.

If your prospect says no, answer, "I understand. If it's okay, I'd like to call back. What time would be most convenient for you?" Your prospect is either going to give you a better time to call or they will ask what your call is all about. This gives you an opening to continue.

If your prospect gives you another time to call, call back at that time and continue your script. If they ask, "What is this about?" begin your meeting presentation by tying in how and why Jim Smith suggested you call. The weight of the influence of Jim Smith will show, based on the interest of your prospect. Remember that this call is to make a meeting, not to make a sales presentation. As you answer any questions your prospect may have, always remind them that you can only get more specific once you get together.

Now you're at the third part of the Prospect Agreement. The last question you always ask is similar to your negotiation question at the end of the sales presentation. "Which would be better for you, Monday at 10 A.M. or Tuesday at 3 P.M.?" Give your prospect a choice. Remember your weekly plan sheet from Part Two? This is where you find the times and days to offer your prospect.

If you were to ask, "When would you like to get together?", this gives them the opportunity to put it off. If you ask, "Would you like to get together?", this gives them the opportunity to say no. Another reason to ask for a specific time is that most individuals do not organize themselves very well. By asking for two specific times, you'll force your prospect into a situation where they need to think and to get themselves organized enough to see you.

One of the major reasons why prospects refuse to talk to you and/or see you is because of the perceived waste of their time. Most individuals are either too busy and/or too unorganized to set a time to see you. Once they feel comfortable that their time won't be wasted, they'll feel more comfortable in meeting with you. Here's an example of the referral telephone contact approach:

1) **Identify yourself and your firm:** "Good morning, this is Sam Stone with ABC Technologies."

2) **Establish rapport:** "John Smith asked that I call. Do you have a moment?"

3) **Make an interest creative comment (build ego):** "John says you have a successful marketing firm."

4) **Briefly introduce what you have or do:** "We work with organizations like yours to dramatically increase sales."

5) **Ask for the meeting:** "To help you better understand what we have, I'd like an opportunity to get together with you. Would Tuesday at 3 P.M. or Wednesday at 10 A.M. be better for you?"

6) **Lock in your meeting:** "What is your correct address?" or "What is the best way to get to your office?"

7) **Confirm meeting:** "I look forward to meeting you Wednesday morning at 10 A.M."

Here's an example of a cold call telephone meeting approach that I used during the years I was selling radio advertising. This approach worked about 75 percent of the time. As a matter of fact, my sales manager used to sit next to me as I was making my calls. After setting a meeting time, using this approach, he would ask, "So what's your great idea to help these prospects?" I told him I wouldn't know until I saw the prospect, because the ideas would come from asking questions (more about this technique in Process Step No. 3):

1) **Identify yourself and your firm:** "Good morning, this is Sam Stone with ABC Technologies."

2) **Briefly introduce what you have or do:** "We work with businesses like yours to increase productivity."

3) **Use a statement to get their interest immediately:** "I help retail firms like yours move merchandise off their shelves. Do you have a moment?"

4) Ask for the meeting.
5) Lock in your meeting.
6) Confirm meeting.

In each of the above examples, if your prospect says "no" to having a moment, simply ask what time would be better, and contact them at that time. Remember that your objective is to set a firm time to get together with your prospect, not to sell anything but just to arrange a meeting time. Should they give you an objection to seeing you, say, "I'd like a few minutes of your time to ask a few questions to determine if what we have would help increase your business. Should you feel our product/service might fill your needs, we'll discuss it in more detail; if not, you might know some other companies that might benefit from what we have. Would 10 A.M. Wednesday be better or . . . ?" (Continue, setting your meeting time.)

What you've accomplished is to let your prospect realize you're not going to waste his/her time, you've given them an out to end the presentation, and you've let them know you'll be asking for referrals. If you don't make a sale, at least you may leave with a few names. (More about getting referrals in Process Step No. 8).

Many salespeople call from a position of weakness. Their belief is that it's rare for a cold call to turn into a sale. They make calls and go through the motions hoping that someone will buy.

Before you make any calls, call from a position of strength. Have absolute belief that the person on the other end of the line wants to buy from you. Write and then read specific verbal statements to yourself about your call. For example:

"I enjoy making phone calls to individuals I have yet to meet."

"Everyone I call wants to talk to and buy from me."

"I am so enthusiastic that no one can help but discuss our product/service with me."

After repeating your statements out loud, begin your calls immediately. It's amazing that when many salespeople have to make phone calls, they fear even picking up the telephone.

How do you become great at making calls? How do you develop the skill level of the highest paid salespeople? Make ten thousand phone calls. If that sounds like a lot, it's only forty dials every day. I made over ten thousand dials every year for five years. I made the calls at the same time every day, and most of the dials could be accomplished in one hour.

Many salespeople have a tremendous amount of time on their hands, as they are doing unimportant tasks during the sales day. If you plan your time correctly and do the same high priority tasks every day (CCDA), you'll have time to make the calls, set the meetings and make the sales.

Two final notes: When making your calls and talking with your prospect and/or leaving messages, be confident and direct. When you're not quite sure that what you're selling will sell or that the prospect will buy, your voice has a sound that lacks confidence. If you're heard this way on the telephone, no matter how hard you try, you won't be able to set a meeting time in order to make the sale.

And be direct. If your prospect feels you're meandering on the phone, they'll also feel that you'll waste their time during the meeting. Develop confidence, be direct and go make sales!

Let's summarize:
1) Use verbal statements before making your calls.
2) When calling anyone, always give your name, company and reason for calling.
3) Always ask permission, no matter whom you are calling.
4) If the party is busy, ask when you should call back.
5) Always call back at the time requested.
6) Use the steps for making calls and don't put the phone down!
7) To become great, make ten thousand calls.

These suggestions aren't complicated, but you'll stand head and shoulders above anyone else making calls. The average salesperson uses the hit or miss method to make phone calls, and the result is usually missed since they end up not making calls at all.

When dealing with people remember you are not dealing with creatures of logic, but with creatures of emotion.

∾ DALE CARNEGIE

Action No. 1: Develop your own script for referrals and cold calls. This is one part of the presentation where you can actually read the script without having to memorize it.

1. Open: _____

_____

2. Introduction: _____

_____

3. Ask for the meeting: _____

_____

_____

4. Lock in the meeting: _____

_____

5. Confirm the time: _____

_____

Action No. 2: Answer the following questions to make sure that every contact pays off!

1. How many calls must I make every day to have ten thousand calls each year?

_____

2. At what time and at what place am I making all of my calls and contacts?

_____

3. Am I asking permission to speak to every contact?

_____

4. Am I using a follow-up system with every contact? (See Step No. 9.)

_____

5. Statements to use before every call (add more of your own):

A) I'm a businessperson calling a businessperson about a business proposition. Therefore, it's easy to set a meeting. My product/service will benefit this person!

B) People are friendly and receptive to me because they know immediately that I like them and I am genuinely interested in them.

C) I like people. People like me and confide in me. This person will be glad to meet me!

D) People are interesting and fascinating. I thoroughly enjoy meeting them!

E) I express myself in terms of my prospect's interests, needs and desires and thereby am persuasive in my words.

F) I am confident and successful on the telephone.

G) I call my prospects and expect positive results.

H) I know what to do on the phone, and I do it daily.

I) I am in the right place at the right time, successfully engaged in the right activity!

J) I change people's lives!

PROCESS STEP NO. 2: THE MEETING – REMOVING THE "GARBAGE CAN LID"

If I listen I have the advantage; if I speak others have it.
∾ FROM THE ARABIC

You've contacted your prospect, the call went well, and you've established a time and place to meet. You've put everything together that you need for your meeting, but what do you do to prepare yourself mentally for this presentation?

Being clearly focused to meet your potential client is as important as what you'll say later when you ask them to buy. Your mental attitude determines how far you'll go with this prospect. Your mental attitude also helps lower the "garbage can lid" to help you "see the whites of their eyes."

Imagine the following scenario: You drive to the prospect's office and park in front. As you get out of your vehicle, the door to your prospect's office opens, and a red carpet rolls out. Two trumpeters now appear on either side of the door as they trumpet your arrival.

As you walk up the red carpet, your prospect comes out, puts his/her arm around your shoulder and escorts you in. As both of you walk toward the door, your prospect says, "I've been waiting all day for you. I'm looking forward to hearing what you have to say so that I can become one of your best clients!"

What would your expectations be of making a sale? That's what I thought. Such a scene will probably never happen, but it must happen in your mind before every meeting with a potential client. Why? The attitude of your prospect will be in direct proportion to the attitude you bring in with you.

What if your prospect's attitude is extremely negative when you arrive? The odds of your turning your prospect's attitude around are much greater when you arrive with a positive attitude, rather than with a less positive one. I've always believed that I'd rather enter a sales presentation feeling I would succeed, than enter a sales presentation believing I would fail.

Use the following statements as you're getting our of your vehicle and before you meet with your prospect:

1) **I'm a great salesperson. No one has a greater right to talk to this person than I do. I've been sent to see this person by someone they respect. I use controlled attention, concentrated energy and sustained effort. I have empathy for them, compassion for them and I care for them as human beings. I can see through**

their eyes the benefits that I know they will receive from working with me. I'll enter this sales situation without giving any consideration to defeat.

2) **What's behind this door I do not know. But this I know and know it well. The more I open the more I sell.**

3) **If I have everything to gain and nothing to lose by trying, I'll by all means try.**

4) **I'll do it now!**

(SUCCESS MOTIVATION INSTITUTE, WACO, TX)

Repeating these words guides your unconscious mind to focus on the business at hand, regardless of your attitude. Let's say your day has not been going well, and you have a negative attitude. As you approach your prospect's door, take out the imaginary plastic bag you carry with you for occasions such as these. Open the plastic bag and fill it with all of the negative thoughts you currently have in your head. Take the bag and hang it on the outside door handle before you walk in. You're now entering your sales presentation with a 100 percent focus on your prospect, not yourself.

Your total concentration must go toward your prospect, nothing else. Once you meet your prospect, the outside world ends, nothing else is important. Your cell phone is turned off, your pager is off, and you concentrate on your prospect.

This is now the time to help your prospect begin to remove their "garbage can lid." To begin your trust and relationship development, once you first meet your prospect, you'll need to spend no less than five minutes breaking the ice. During this time, you're asking questions about his/her office, how they know your referral or something about their business.

Not only is this designed to help get their "lid" down, but it's also designed to make you more comfortable before you begin your formal selling process so that you can "see the whites of their eyes." By spending this time with your new prospect, you're beginning to trust each other because you're getting to know each other. You're also not ready to sell yet. You need to set the stage and the pace of the selling process. It's your sale, not the prospect's sale!

By the way, once you leave the prospect's office, whether you've made the sale or not, forget that invisible plastic bag that's holding all of your negative thoughts and emotions . . . you don't need it anyway!

"Garbage can lid" statements from your prospect tell you that you still can't "see the whites of their eyes." As mentioned in Part One, the following are the verbal equivalents to the "garbage can lid:"

"Just give me your best price!"
"I only have ten minutes!"
"I can't make any decisions without my partner/spouse!"
"I'm just looking!"

What happens if you agree with any of these statements? Your prospect will never become one of your clients because you've made the cardinal error in selling. The error is to let your prospect remain in control. The salesperson should always be in control, but the client must always feel like they're in control!

How do you accomplish that? By asking questions or by answering a question with a question. You need to understand how to ask these questions with a little finesse and psychology. There are four communication processes. They are:

Reading
Writing
Speaking
Listening

In school, we focused on reading and writing. Some of us might have even had a little training in the art of speaking. But most of us had no training in how to listen.

As adults, the communication process is reversed. These days, we rarely read or write but spend most of our day speaking and listening. As a matter of fact, the majority of our day is spent listening rather than speaking. So, of all the communication skills we use, the one we use the most, the one that makes us the most money is the one that we were never taught to use.

We should use listening as a way to lead the prospect to what it is they're looking for. And this is probably one of the most important keys. Prospects hate spending money and making decisions. But they enjoy buying items and having salespeople help them to make decisions.

Closing is not the art of getting a person to make a decision. Closing is the art of making a decision with which your prospect will agree.

∾ PAUL J. MEYER

Action: Begin to use your "prospect agreement." Write out what each step in the process might sound like:

Set expectations: (e.g., "My name is Sam Stone, nice meeting you. Thank you for the time to meet with you. What I'd like to do is find out more about your business.")

_____

Do what you say you will do: (e.g., "Your friend John Smith says you've known each other for ten years. Have you been in this business that long?)

_____

Gain agreement: (e.g., "I'd like to ask a few questions regarding yourself and your business. Is that all right?")

_____

PROCESS STEP NO. 3: THE INTERVIEW — FINDING THE "GAP"

No man likes to feel that he is being sold something or to do a thing.
We much prefer to feel that we are buying of our own accord or acting on our own
ideas. We like to be consulted about our wishes, our wants, our thoughts.

∾ DALE CARNEGIE

This is the step in the sales process where you'll be spending time finding out what your prospect wants. But even more importantly, this step in the process lets your prospect feel better about you. Here's why: When you let someone else speak, and you listen intently, letting him or her feel you're interested, psychologically, the other person feels closer to you. They usually don't realize it's happening, and they don't know why. Their "shield" is now beginning to come down.

This is the most important part of the sales process. The more effectively you spend time with your prospect, the easier the rest of the sales presentation will unfold, and the more money you'll make.

During the first part of my career in the training business, I was selling sales training packages. Each presentation was targeted at sixty minutes. The first five minutes was the warm-up, the next thirty minutes consisted of the consultation/qualifying stage.

We're now thirty-five minutes into a sixty-minute presentation, and the prospect has yet to see the package. Remember that all I had to sell was this package. If the prospect didn't qualify or I wasn't able to get buying motives during this stage, I wouldn't have a sale and wouldn't make any money.

The next fifteen minutes was spent showing the prospect how this package would solve the problems uncovered (the "gap") during the previous phase. The last ten minutes was spent asking the prospect to buy. The sixty-minute presentation was successful because of the time spent during the consultation/qualifying stage. Your success as a salesperson is directly dependent on the amount of time and quality of this stage (the "interview").

The "interview" is one of the most misunderstood, yet important parts of the sales process. Here is where you are receiving not only the information to sell your prospect, but more importantly, the trust and confidence of your prospect. Here is where you "see the whites of their eyes!" Spending time with your prospect up-front is equivalent to increasing your odds of making a sale.

Imagine the entire sales presentation much like a pyramid (illustration #1).

On the first level is the meeting. Next might be the interview. Third would be the presentation, and, finally, on the bottom is the negotiation.

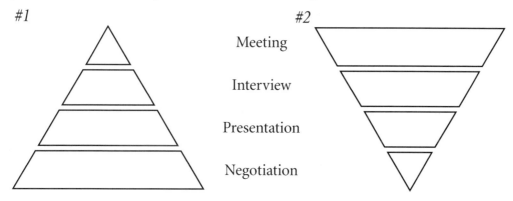

#1

#2

Meeting

Interview

Presentation

Negotiation

With a sales pyramid looking like illustration #1, the salesperson spends very little time up-front getting to know the prospect and their needs. By the time the salesperson asks the prospect to buy, the process is long, drawn out and the focus is generally on price. You can make the sale, but you lose profit and probably your client, because they won't be back or buy from you again.

Now imagine the same pyramid, but inverted (illustration #2). The salesperson is spending most of the time at the top, getting to know the prospect and the prospect's needs. Since the salesperson has gotten close to the prospect, and the prospect trusts the salesperson, not only can the sale be made, but the prospect's question during the negotiation step is "how soon can I get it," not "how low a price will you offer me."

Salespeople who approach the sale by spending little time getting to know their prospect have a very poor idea of what the prospect is looking for. As a result, these salespeople have a very difficult time negotiating and when they do, either the prospect buys at a very small margin and/or the prospect fights the salesperson all the way to the sale.

Salespeople who approach the sale as an inverted pyramid spend time up-front to get to know the prospect and attempt to understand why and what the prospect is looking for. As a result, by the time the salesperson is ready to negotiate the sale, the question is not "if," but "how" and "when."

In fact, you must sell yourself so well that your customers feel ashamed
to even think about doing business with someone else.

☙ "WE ALL SELL . . . BUT SOME SELL BETTER. WHY?" BY ROBERT L. SHOOK

Action: How is your pyramid positioned? Write down what percentage of the time you should spend in each step of the sales process.

The Meeting: _____%

The Interview: _____%

The Presentation: _____%

The Negotiation: _____%

The Reassurance: _____%

The Delivery: _____%

Qualifying the Prospect

The mere act of asking can be the main difference between one person's success and another person's station in life.

∾ ROBERT RINGER

One of the best ways to gain control in a sales situation and to qualify your prospect is to ask questions. When you're asking questions, you're in control. But, something else also happens when you ask questions. You're making your prospect feel good about you. When your prospect is speaking, they feel good about expressing who they are, while you are sitting back and listening, finding out about their self-image. Their "lid" is coming down!

In addition, they are telling you what they want. You can't present your product or service until they tell you what they want. They'll tell you exactly what they want to buy just by asking the right questions.

We were told growing up that we should never answer a question with a question. My suggestion is to change that statement and answer all questions with a question. If your prospect asks you a question, you can always respond with "Why?" or "Why do you say that?" When your prospect asks you a question, they have now gained control of the sales presentation.

What do you do if you catch yourself making a statement, rather than a question? Add, "Would you agree?" or "Isn't that correct?" to the end of your statement. But make sure that you are constantly asking questions. Asking questions should always be a part of your sales arsenal.

What you're doing is qualifying by asking questions. "What do you want?" "How do you want it?" "When do you want it?" "Why do you want it?"

The profession where professionals ask these types of questions is news reporting. When you are in front of a prospect or client, you are a reporter writing a story. This story is about what you are going to help your prospect achieve by using your product or service.

Many salespeople believe the prospect knows what he/she wants. Sometimes that's true, but in most cases, the prospect will never have all the information and background that you have about the product or service they're purchasing. At this point, you become a consultant to your prospect. The more time you take with this prospect to find out what it is he/she wants and needs, the more they psychologically become attuned to you and trust you to help them in the sales process . . . you're "seeing the whites of their eyes!"

How do you do all of this? If at all possible, position yourself and the prospect physically in a situation where you have total control. If you sell by phone, this will be difficult, but you always want to make yourself as comfortable as possible with few, if any, distractions.

If you're in a situation where your prospect is coming to you, have them sit in a comfortable chair, offer them a cup of coffee and make them feel as if they are guests in your home. In many retail situations, this would be very difficult to do, but you can always offer a cup of coffee or a drink of water and make them feel comfortable.

If you're an outside salesperson, sit at a table where the prospect is at your dominant writing hand. For instance, if you're right-handed, make sure you sit to your prospect's left side. This way, as you write, you can work closely with your prospect.

At a restaurant, always make sure you ask for a four-top, a square table with four chairs. This table has much more room to be comfortable. Your wait-person will want to put you at a two-top, so they can leave the larger tables open for larger parties, but if you ask, you'll probably get the larger table, if available. If at all possible, stay away from booths. These situations make it extremely awkward to make a presentation and a sale. Here, you're sitting across from your prospect and have very little room and are possibly cramped.

In an office situation, if at all possible sit next to your prospect. Pull a chair around their desk (with their permission) or sit at a conference table. By physically getting close to your prospect (as opposed to sitting across from one another), you're letting your prospect pull their "garbage can lid" down so you can begin the trust relationship.

Qualifying your prospect in this way is one of the most critical areas of your sales presentation. Here is where the sale is made. Here is where trust begins by helping them with their "garbage can lid." Here is where your next sale begins; and here is where you begin to receive referrals.

This doesn't all happen at the same time, but if this part of your presentation isn't right on track, the sales won't be made, and nothing else matters after that.

You're looking for the true motive to buy, in addition to their capability to buy. Remember, the motive is never the desire to own your product or service, it's the desire to have whatever your product/service does for or gives to your prospect. This is true salesmanship. It's finding out whatever it is your prospect wants and helping your prospect get more of it.

Asking questions is the most important skill you'll develop and one that will continue throughout your entire career. The key to asking questions is to develop a strong focus on your prospect. Probing questions make the prospect think about what they hadn't thought about before. These are the questions that make the sale.

Reporters such as those on "60 Minutes" have developed a fine-tuned skill to ask the right questions to get their interviewee to talk freely as they never have before. This skill is using "open-ended" questions.

"Open-ended" questions are those your prospect has to respond to with a thoughtful answer. Such questions get your prospect to think about subjects they had never thought of before. Here's where you're beginning to gain the prospect's trust.

> Here are a few "open-ended" questions:
> What are you looking for in a new home?
> Why is this the first place you've looked?
> How will you be using this new product?

You'll notice that each of these questions causes your prospect to think about the answer. The more in-depth open-ended questions you ask, the closer you're getting to the sale.

As I work with salespeople around the country, I first notice that they want to get through this part of the sales presentation as quickly as possible to get to the "meat" of the presentation. As a result, they use "closed-ended " questions to get to the client's bottom line as quickly as possible.

"Closed-ended" questions begin to narrow the prospect's comments until you have a specific answer. These are generally used after your initial "open-ended" questions. There's nothing wrong in using closed-ended questions. What's wrong is where they are used.

> Here are a few "closed-ended" questions:
> Which one do you want?
> Will you be using this tool today?
> Is this the first store you've been to?

You can see that these questions give you a "yes," "no" or one word answer. Questions such as these do very little for you, as you attempt to develop trust with your prospect. You can't even "see their eyes!"

You should develop a list of "open-ended" probing questions to use during the interview. (When you open your binder to begin asking questions during your interview, have your list of "planned" questions inside the cover. Nerves, fear and excitement can get you off track. By having these questions nearby, you'll always know what to ask next.) Start with possibly five to ten areas and then develop sub-questions to fill in the gaps.

"Closed-ended" questions can be used toward the end of the interview to move to the next step. These are referred to as "summary" questions.

"Summary" questions do two things for you. First, these questions make sure that you've hit all the points that need to be covered during your presentation.

"Mr. Smith. It looks like you're interested in this, this, this and this, is that correct?" Secondly, you've asked permission to continue and showed that you were listening, all in one closed-ended question.

Selling ain't tellin', it's askin'!

Ꮬ AUTHOR UNKNOWN

Action: Early in my sales career, I developed a list of questions that I kept near-by since occasionally I would lose track of what I wanted to ask a prospect. Develop ten "open-ended" questions to begin to qualify your prospect and gain their trust. Next, add five "closed-ended" summary questions that you can use during your sales interview. Once you've honed down your list to the key questions, commit them to memory.

Open-Ended Questions

1. _____

2. _____

3. _____

4. _____

5. _____

6. _____

7. _____

8. _____

9. _____

10. _____

Closed-Ended Questions

1. _____

2. _____

3. _____

4. _____

5. _____

The Gap

Sales is the only profession that's dedicated to helping people make their dreams come true.

    ∾ WILL RYAN

The "gap" is the spread between where your prospect is now and where you want your prospect to be. In other words, to buy your product or service. Most of the time, your prospect has no idea there's any gap at all. In fact, advertisers help us (the prospect) find the "gap." They let us know there's a gap between where we are now and where they think we should be. So we go out and buy their product. They do this in such a way that makes us want to bridge this gap.

Your persuasive power is in how you ask questions to get your prospect thinking about how bad the pain is by not having the gap filled.

You may have heard of witch doctors in some primitive areas that are capable of getting their "patients" to believe something bad will happen in their life. Their minds are receptive to what they hear because they believe and trust in their "doctor."

Your situation is much the same. By the way you ask questions, you can develop tremendous rapport with your prospect. Asking the right questions that make your prospect think allows them to drop their "shield" or "garbage can lid" and allows them to open up to you so that you can "see the whites of their eyes!" You can then help them understand the need for your product/service, even though they hadn't considered it previously. You simply have to help them understand how they can't live without it. You do this by asking the correct "open-ended" questions.

Once you have answered their questions, you simply present your product/service, and since you've asked the questions so well, your prospect says something like, "That's exactly what I need. How did you know that's what I wanted?" It's similar to a police sketch artist drawing the picture of the perpetrator, turning it around for the victim to see, and the victim says, "That's him, that's the one who did it." You and the police sketch artist are doing exactly the same thing. You both ask questions in such a way to help the person you're with see what's in their mind.

Once discovered, it's almost like magic. You'll notice we're talking about wants, not needs. Needs take care of themselves. The need for clothing, food, water, or shelter is so basic that your prospect makes sure those are taken care of before the "wants" surface.

Our needs are actually very few, but our wants can number into the thousands. What's interesting is that once a want is satisfied and becomes a part of our lives, in our mind, it becomes a need. How many people would live their life without a garage door opener once they have one? Or how about a microwave oven? Would you be willing to cook without one? I had a client who once refused to turn her TV on if she couldn't find the remote control!

The average salesperson sells materials or services.
The creative salesperson sells growth and profit insurance.

❧ AUTHOR UNKNOWN

Action: What do your clients and prospects want? Think back over your last few presentations and write down a few. This will help you understand what to look for and what questions to ask as you work with your new prospects.

1. _____

2. _____

3. _____

4. _____

5. _____

Owning Your Prospect's Problems

To be trusted is a greater compliment than to be loved.

∾ GEORGE MACDONALD

Trust is the highest level of communication afforded by a client in a business situation. Once you've developed trust with your prospect, you can sell them anything you want. But don't let this go to your head. There's a tremendous amount of responsibility attached to a trust relationship. Not only can you sell your prospect anything you want, but you also need to make sure that what you are selling to your prospect is right for them.

The equivalent to trust in a family is love. You can't take this to any higher level. You either love/trust someone or you don't. But again, there's a tremendous amount of responsibility attached to both love and trust.

One of the key areas in the minds of your prospects where trust is paramount is in taking care of their problems. Not only do your prospects want you to be responsible for their problem, they also want you to prove to them how good you really are.

You develop this responsibility when you position yourself as the only person who can take care of their problem. You should become so good at what you do (both selling your prospect and taking care of your client) that your prospect wouldn't ever consider doing business with anyone else. This is where you begin to add value to your relationship with this prospect. This is where the trust begins; this is where you "see the whites of their eyes!"

Whenever a problem occurs because of something your client has purchased from you, you are in a unique position to show them how good you are as you take care of them. When everything goes right, your client can trust you, but when something goes wrong, the trust begins to slip, and the client begins to watch you and what moves you'll make next. This is a critical time.

Should you do the wrong things or worse, do nothing, your client sees you as an opportunist, simply wanting to take their money in exchange for the product or service you sold them.

On the other hand, when you do more for your client, they see you as someone who's looking out for them, a fairy godparent so to speak. Once your client sees you as their hero, you've joined the ranks of the trusted sales professional. These are your loyal clients. They'll buy anything from you. They trust you to take care of them and to look out for them. You're their super hero!

How important are you to your clients? Let's put it this way: Prospects want someone to take care of them. Your clients will be sending you referrals continually because they want their friends to become a part of their great fortune. This client has now become a "center of influence" (more about "centers of influence" in step 8). They'll send leads to you, and these new prospects will buy simply because your original client trusts you. This trust is transferable. But you must treat this trust correctly.

If you abuse this trust with these new clients, your original client will find out, and the trust you developed with your original client will be gone forever.

He who is master of himself will win the confidence of others.
∾ AUTHOR UNKNOWN

Action: What are you doing to "own" your prospect's problems? What are you doing for your clients that is out of the ordinary and says to your prospect "I'm the one to take care of your problem better than anyone else"? Think of a specific situation where you began to "own" their problem. Why did they begin to trust you?

Client Motivation

A diamond is simply a chunk of coal that made good under pressure.
◦ AUTHOR UNKNOWN

The number one job of the sales consultant is to find a way for the prospect to say yes. You do this by changing the motivation of your prospect.

Here's why this is so important and potentially difficult. Do you have any habit that you know you should change but are doing nothing about it? My guess is that your answer is probably yes. Therefore, if *you* have a habit that you're not changing and you know *you* should, how easy will it be to get your prospect to change their current buying habits and start buying from you?

Also, have you ever been with a negative prospect? Who's supposed to change whose attitude? It has to be you! Attitudes and motivation are contagious. If you let your prospects control the way you think and act, you've lost and they've sold you. On the other hand, if you can help them change from a negative attitude to a positive attitude, you're 90 percent closer to making the sale.

You've heard of "motivational speakers." Actually there is no such animal. In reality, speakers can't motivate somebody else; only you can motivate you. You are the only individual capable of causing attitudinal change. What you must do with your prospect is to "inspire" change by pulling from them the information necessary for their change. What's interesting is that very few people understand or are capable of doing this. This amounts to a three-step question process:

1) Ask your prospect where they'd like to be two years from now.
2) Ask what they'll do differently, beginning today, that will help them get to where they'd like to be in two years.
3) Finally, ask how they'll begin doing this new activity.

You're asking questions that either your prospect doesn't have the answers to (since they really haven't thought them through yet) or they have to really think about. This is how change occurs, and by asking these questions you're becoming their change agent!

People can be divided into three groups: those who make things happen, those who watch things happen, and those who wonder what happened.

∾ JOHN W. NEWBERN

Action: How will you "motivate" yourself to "motivate" or inspire others? Write down five questions that you can ask your prospect to help them understand how to begin changing themselves and therefore become your client:

1. _____

2. _____

3. _____

4. _____

5. _____

PROCESS STEP NO. 4: THE PRESENTATION – CLOSING THE "GAP"

Don't sell the steak, sell the sizzle.

∾ ELMER LETTERMAN

Any selling must be oriented toward what your prospect wants, *not what you want*. You want a sale and the rewards that come along with that sale. But most importantly, if you focus on your prospect's point-of-view, wants take care of themselves. You receive your rewards and your prospect becomes your client.

Your focus should always be on the benefits, the sizzle, and not the features, the steak. Your prospect doesn't care about what you're selling, they care about what's in it for them.

Your prospect could care less about what you're selling:
> Prospects don't care about air bags in their automobile; they care about being able to walk away from an accident.
> Prospects don't care about life insurance; they care about their loved ones being financially stable should they die prematurely.
> And prospects don't care about the clothes you're selling; they care about how they'll look wearing them.

Let's begin our discussion of the "presentation" by understanding why Features, Advantages and Benefits (FABs) work to increase sales for you.
> A feature is what your product or service is.
> An advantage is what it does.
> And a benefit is what it will do for your client.

For example, let's discuss windshield wipers. What is a windshield wiper? It's a piece of rubber. That's the feature, in other words what it is. What's the advantage? It clears water away during a rainstorm. That's what it does. What's the benefit to your client? It lets them drive home safely during a downpour. That's very simple. Your client is buying safety, the benefit, and not a piece of rubber.

The problem is that most salespeople sell the advantage not the benefit. What most salespeople say is "Mr. and Mrs. Prospect, a windshield wiper is simply a piece of rubber that will clear away the rain while you're driving!"

What was left out? The benefit! Most salespeople give the prospect an implied benefit, assuming the prospect will understand what the benefit is. They don't! You must tell them, because the benefit is what they are buying.

Again, your prospects don't care about airbags in cars, insurance policies, clothing, etc.; they are buying what these features will do for them . . . the benefits!

Here's how you would correctly sell windshield wipers. "Mr. and Mrs. Prospect, a windshield wiper is simply a piece of rubber that will clear away the rain while you're driving. What this means to you is that you will be able to drive home in a downpour!"

Remember the phrase just used, "What this means to you is . . . !" This is a transition phrase that forces you to give your client the true value of the feature of this product or service. To make sure you have given them the real benefit (because sometimes there are a number of benefits for any given product), you need to use the "so what" test.

The "so what" test helps you to drill down to the true benefit. When you can't come up with any other answer, you've passed the "so what" test. For example, when you tell the prospect that they'll look great wearing those new clothes, you may be able to add additional benefits by saying "so what." If that's the case you haven't passed the test yet. Keep asking "so what?" until you find the true benefit.

To begin selling benefits, it's imperative that the focus be on value rather than price. Since there is no such thing as a price buyer, it's evident that your client will spend more money with you if you sell value and not price. You do that by focusing on the benefits.

Let's say that you are selling a widget, and the client believes the price is greater than the value. At this point, no matter what you do, you won't sell the prospect. What many salespeople do to get the client to buy is to lower the price, hoping at some point the price will be lower than the value, and the client will buy.

In reality, what happens is that the lower you drop the price, the lower the value becomes in the prospect's mind. Why is that? The prospect psychologically believes that the worth of the product begins to diminish if you keep lowering the price.

So what do you do? Raise the value. How do you do that? Go back to what we just discussed and keep the focus on the benefits. What if the prospect keeps going back to price? Then the prospect is sold, but they haven't given you their buying motives because they may not really know them that well. You job is to pull the buying motives out of them. You do that by asking the correct "open-ended" questions.

Value to your prospect means that what they receive is greater than what they pay. Assuming you can't change the price of your product or service, then you are the one that helps the prospect understand that the benefits are much greater than the cost.

Bait the hook to suit the fish.

ɷ DALE CARNEGIE

Action: What are your FABs? Develop advantages and benefits to five of your key features. Remember that your prospects and clients buy benefits, not advantages. A feature is what it is, an advantage is what it does and a benefit is why it's important to your prospect.

Feature	Advantage	Benefit
(What it is)	(What it does)	(Why it's important to your prospect)
1.		
2.		
3.		
4.		
5.		

Facilitation

Have more than thou showest, speak less than thou knowest.
∾ WILLIAM SHAKESPEARE

As a professional, I've worked hard at becoming a facilitator rather than a trainer. The difference is that the trainer gives information to the audience, and the facilitator pulls information from them. The trainer spends most of his/her time talking; the facilitator spends time asking questions. Basically, a facilitator is a salesperson while in front of a group. In other words, a facilitator is a group presenter.

As a facilitator, you are in control. When you are in control, you make the sale. You gain control by asking questions. The audience answering your questions feels like they are in control, because they're participating in the process. In front of your group, you are a leader. Leaders ask questions, control the group and take command by your presence.

By gaining psychological control of your audience, you are in an enviable position to increase your sales dramatically. But remember, the key to your success is not only by asking questions that pull the right information from your audience, but also by asking the right questions. You will be able to ask the right ones by knowing your audience.

Here's a trick I used whenever I was to sell to a group. I got together with some of the top salespeople who would be in the audience; individuals, who I was told, were very open to change. I made a mini-presentation to them to get them presold prior to the event. Not only did this help me understand my audiences better, but I also had allies in the audience at the time of negotiation.

It's necessary to learn individual sales before attempting group sales. It's just as important to speak to one person as it is to speak in front of your group. Don't make a presentation to twenty people. You're actually making your presentation to one person twenty times . . . at the same time!

When I began selling training programs, the focus was on one-on-one selling. I was booking five meetings each day, seeing four of those meetings, asking three to buy, selling one and getting twenty referrals. Making a sale a day was okay, but the activity level became overwhelming.

When I realized I could make as much during one presentation as I could in one day, my interest was aroused. The major difference is that you must be very detailed about your planning. It's imperative that you have all the tools you need and that you are totally prepared about every phase of your presentation. It isn't just that you are making one presentation to twenty people, you are making twenty presentations to twenty people at one time. Multiplying these intangibles is incredible.

You need to be able to read your entire audience individually as you are making your presentation. To be able to do that, you must know your material backwards and forwards in such a way that no matter where you are within your presentation, no matter what happens during your presentation, you can react immediately. At this point, you must be able to deal with the situation and get back on track without missing a beat.

This takes practice. The more group presentations you make and the more experience you receive, the better you get. Don't dismiss making individual one-on-one presentations. The highest paid group presenters are also excellent individual presenters. This occurs because when you make presentations one-on-one you begin to understand how an individual thinks and reacts. This is imperative if you are to make group presentations. Without this skill, you will have no idea how the group is reacting and therefore will lose everyone.

The way to build self-confidence is to start
doing things you're not sure you can do.
ల AUTHOR UNKNOWN

Action: A great facilitator becomes great by understanding how to ask the correct questions in front of a group. What five questions would you ask to gain control with a group? To be better prepared, write out these five potential questions. (Example: Who would have interest in doubling their income?):

1. _____

2. _____

3. _____

4. _____

5. _____

PROCESS STEP NO. 5: THE NEGOTIATION

The average salesperson closes twice. The average client buys after the third close.
 ∾ AUTHOR UNKNOWN

After you've finished asking questions and you have the information you need, you now are at the point at which you have the information necessary to tell your prospect how they can achieve what they want through the methods you have.

The next step is to ask for the order. Remember that the more time you spend with your prospect in the interview step, less time is needed and more trust is present during the negotiation. In reality, the negotiation began when you began the selling process. All the things you've accomplished up to this point influence what will happen next. The negotiation is smooth because you can "see the whites of their eyes!"

Most sales training programs refer to this step as "the close!" I'd prefer to refer to it as "the negotiation." "Closing" refers to something coming to an end. This process is actually the beginning of a relationship.

"Negotiation" doesn't mean "will they buy?" but rather, "how much, or when will they buy?" I'd rather enter this phase of the sales process wondering how and when the prospect buys rather than wondering "if" the prospect will buy. The term "closing" means the salesperson has some trepidation at this step.

"Negotiation" means the salesperson has total confidence that he or she will satisfy the prospect enough for them to become a new client. Negotiation is also a give and take from both parties. This follows as you develop your relationship earlier in your presentation.

Here are your three criteria questions you should ask:
   1) "If what I have could help you get the results you want to achieve,"
   2) "If what I have fits within the time constraints (if you have the time to do/use it),"
   3) "If what I have would fit within the budget you've set aside, is there any reason why you wouldn't take action today?"

It's better to close too early and too often than too seldom and too late!
 ∾ PAUL J. MEYER

This statement has been proven true time after time as salespeople continually fail to make money by not getting the sale. In most sales situations, the prospect does not say, "I'll take it!" As a matter of fact, they probably won't say it because they believe your job is to ask for the order.

But what do you say to get your prospect to buy? You've made an excellent presentation based on the needs and wants of your prospect. It's almost like a well-rehearsed play. You're now entering the final scene. The build-up has been tremendous, you know the prospect wants to buy. But you don't know what to say or how to say it. You stumble and fall. The last scene has ruined the entire play.

As I work with salespeople, I often ask them to recite their negotiation question to me. Their response is either "It's whatever I think of at the time," or "I let the prospect decide when to buy." Both comments lead to the scenario above. The salesperson has ruined a great performance, and the prospect's "lid" goes back up.

Every sales presentation is different, as every negotiation situation is different. The negotiation needs to be customized to fit the prospect. But, you must develop a method that will appeal to the majority of your prospects. This method must be written out and memorized so that the entire production flows smoothly, while giving you and therefore the prospect, confidence. As mentioned, it's the last scene of the play.

Once written and memorized, the negotiation will be much smoother since there's no need to think about what to say. The focus is now on your prospect, not on what you have to say. Since it's memorized, it's also easier to vary from the script and customize it to the prospect and the situation.

For example: "It's obvious you understand and appreciate the benefits of this product or service. So the only questions you probably have are how much does it cost and how soon can you get it or start it. Is that correct? You'll always be happy with this product or service. The benefits we discussed will continue throughout the life of this product or service. Which would be easier for you, our monthly payment plan of "X" dollars each month or would you like to put the total of "X" dollars on you credit card?"

A statement similar to this, if memorized, lets you watch your prospect and anticipate how they will react and what you may have to do to overcome any objections.

Prospects hate doing two things: making decisions and spending money. Prospects enjoy having decisions made for them and buying things. You have allowed your prospect to have the major decision made for them. All they have to do is to make a minor decision as to time. You also let them buy without the need to spend money.

It has been said that after you ask the negotiation question you should "SHUT UP!" And that the first person to speak loses. If this were true, then the prospect who says "I'll take it" after answering this question has just lost. How could a new client who speaks first and who agrees to buy a product or service meant to be of a benefit lose? They can't! The first person who speaks is the winner!

You may feel uncomfortable waiting for the prospect to speak first, but let them. You may feel you are putting pressure on the prospect at this point. Yes, pressure is present, but you are not applying it. The prospect is allowing pressure to be there, and the prospect is applying it, you're not.

Throughout the entire sales presentation, you've told the prospect about all the benefits of your product or service. The prospect, if sold correctly, can't wait to buy.

But then you ask the negotiation question and ask your prospect to spend money.

At this point, all the benefits you've gotten your prospect to agree to are forgotten in favor of having to make a decision and spend money. All the reasons why they should buy have evaporated into thin air.

You now have to remind the prospect of all the benefits of your product or service. You do this by asking questions such as, "Do you remember how you said you'd feel when you used this? ..."

Your prospect has now been reminded of the benefits available by purchasing your product/service. You assumed your prospect would buy by the tense of the statement. You asked the prospect to buy by assuming the sale was completed. You simply let them buy and not decide if or when they would buy.

There is no middle ground, either you sell your prospect or he sells you.

∾ JIM CLARK

Action: What do you say to your prospect during this "negotiation" phase of the sales process? Write out the words you use, or would like to use, to get your prospect to agree and to buy.

Always Negotiate on Something

Always leave them wanting more.
ↆ GEORGE M. COHAN

Most sales presentations do not end with the client buying but with some other ending; the prospect wants to think about it; you need to get back together with them again, etc.

Make sure that whenever you're with a prospect and the meeting ends for whatever reason, including the prospect buying, that you "negotiate" on something!

"Negotiating" means asking the prospect to buy, but since that doesn't always happen, you must remain in control of the selling situation and "negotiate" on some next event.

For instance, you've made your first presentation to the potential client, and another meeting is needed. Negotiate when that next meeting will be.

Your potential client needs to discuss your suggestions with someone else. Negotiate when they'll meet or when you can meet with both of them.

If this potential client won't buy or doesn't qualify for some reason, negotiate on referrals.

You're on the phone with your client. Negotiate when your next meeting will happen.

The bottom line is that the salesperson who continually negotiates at the end of every contact not only has control of the selling situation, but also control of his/her time and income.

The great end of life is not knowledge but action.
ↆ ALDOUS HUXLEY

Action: Do you "negotiate" at every opportunity? Write down what questions you'll ask when another meeting or contact is needed or to receive referrals.

1. _____

2. _____

3. _____

4. _____

5. _____

PROCESS STEP NO. 6: THE REASSURANCE – HANDLING OBJECTIONS

Nothing will be attempted if all possible objections must be first overcome.

∾ SAMUEL JOHNSON

In many sales situations, prospects have questions about the potential sale. Many salespeople see these as objections. Objections are simply questions from your prospect about why they should buy. Your prospect is looking for reassurance. Should you, for some reason, not sell your prospect at this point (and it happens more times than not), you'll go back to a previous step such as the interview or the presentation.

If your prospect should object, you'll want to make sure you use a five-step approach to turning objections into sales.

First of all, if you're getting the same objections on a regular basis, make sure to bring the objection up early in the presentation. For instance, if you receive the objection that the size of your product is too large, bring this situation up early in the sales process and deal with it before your prospect mentions it. By mentioning the situation before the prospect has a chance to, your prospect will believe that this is not a problem since you're willing to address it.

Secondly, early in the presentation is a great time to deal with objections. Either you get through them and have a quicker negotiation or you find out that the objection is a problem that can't be overcome and you save both you and your prospect a lot of time. Additionally, there are only about four or five objections you receive from prospects on a regular basis. Three of these objections include:

a) Lack of time
b) Money
c) Time to think

Figure out what these objections are and develop a plan for handling them, either when you bring them up or when your prospect does.

Here are the five steps to turn objections into sales:
1) Listen carefully to the objection
2) Acknowledge and agree with your prospect
3) Restate the objection (negative) into a question (positive)
4) Answer the question
5) Confirm the sale

Let's take each one individually.

1) **Listen carefully.** If you were to count the number of objections you receive, you would find that very few are about your product or service. But you're probably receiving the same objections over and over, which is why you should follow the suggestion above—bring them up early.

The problem is not what the objection is, but why the prospect is raising it. By not listening, you're deciding how you're going to answer the objection based on all the answers you've given in the past, but it may be the wrong answer to the right objection.

A story illustrates this situation. A realtor is showing a home to a couple, and the husband asks, "Is there enough room in this home for my mother-in-law to live with us?"

Eager to make the sale the realtor replies, "Absolutely, there's plenty of room!" "Well, I don't want it then," the husband says. "I don't want my mother-in-law living with us!"

This story illustrates how the realtor handled an objection, but she didn't realize it was an objection because she jumped to a conclusion before getting all the information and listening. What the realtor should have asked was "Are you looking for a home large enough for your mother-in-law to live with you?" If she received a negative answer, she would have had the correct information to proceed with the presentation rather than lose it.

Which brings up a point. Rarely should you answer a question directly but rather with another question. There are a number of ways to do this, mostly wrong, as we discussed earlier. But by asking a question, you remain in control of the sales situation, as the realtor could have done in the last example.

2) **Acknowledge and agree with the prospect.** Now that you've listened carefully and heard the objection, agree with your prospect as if you were in their situation. This puts you on their side. It's difficult for your prospect to have negative feelings toward you when you accept what they have to say. It's almost as if you psychologically put your arm around them and said, "It's all right!"

Here's an example: "You're right, spending $500 is a lot of money." Notice you agreed to their feeling of spending money, not to the objection. What your prospect wants at this point is reassurance. They want you to empathize with them, in other words, understand their feelings.

A word of caution: DO NOT USE THE WORDS "BUT" OR "HOWEVER!" During the pause between agreeing with your prospect and the next step, there will be a short silence. Let it happen. This is adding psychological weight to your agreement. As soon as you use the word "but," you've negated your agreement, and your prospect will become defensive. When you use the word "but," you're saying, "I said I agreed with you, but I really don't!"

3) Restate the objection and turn it into a question. When a prospect objects, they're interested or they wouldn't object. They're saying, "Okay, I think I'll buy, but answer this one question before I do." They're not sure or they don't want to spend too much or they don't want to appear foolish to their friends by making an incorrect buying decision. You're here to reassure them.

An example would be a child on a diving board, getting ready to jump in for the first time. Mom or Dad is in the water waiting for the child to jump. The child begins to tell the parent all the reasons for not diving in. The parent keeps repeating that it's okay, that they'll be there to catch the child. That's your part; you're the reassuring parent.

If the objection is "it costs too much," your prospect is really saying, "I want it, but I'd like to pay less." So your response is, "In other words, if the price was less you'd buy it today, is that correct?" What you have done here is to rephrase what your prospect has said (if that's not a correct statement, they'll correct you, so you keep rephrasing until you get agreement).

When you get agreement from your prospect, you've isolated the objection and turned it into the form of a question to be answered. You've also proven to them that you've been listening.

4) Answer the question. Prospects like to buy things and have decisions made for them. They don't like to spend money and make decisions. Here is where you make the buying decision easy for them. Answering the question is not a matter of giving information but asking a series of questions to help the prospect decide why it's so important to own your product or service.

The questions you're asking now are of two types:
   a) Questions they have to think about
   b) Questions they don't have the answers to
For instance: "When was the last time you had a tetanus shot?" (This is probably a question you're not going to ask, unless you're a medical professional, but it's the type of question your prospect would have to think about or wouldn't have an answer to.) By asking the question, your prospect is beginning to sell themselves.

If you had asked the previous question, your prospect may be thinking, "Maybe I really do need that tetanus shot!"

At this point, it's also a matter of reminding your prospect why your product or service was so impressive to them. Remind them of all the reasons why they wanted it in the first place.

Let's go back to the original objection of "it costs too much!" When the prospect agrees with, "In other words, if the price were less you'd buy it today, is that correct?" you follow with questions such as, "What would you like to pay?" or "What do you like most about this product/service?" I like the last one the best because it gets the prospect off of the price and on to the emotional reasons for the purchase. As you progress with these questions, you are essentially into your presentation again. Now you have another chance to negotiate.

5) Confirm the sale. If you fail to negotiate at this point, the prospect begins to object again, and the cycle continues. It's imperative that you ask a negotiation question.

If you follow these five steps every time your prospect objects at any point in your sales presentation, your negotiation average and confidence should improve tremendously.

All master salespeople know that ideas can be sold where merchandise cannot.
Ordinary salespeople don't know this. That is why they are ordinary.

❧ NAPOLEON HILL

Action: Since there are probably only five or so major objections most salespeople encounter, write out each one and write your answer to each objection, using the five-step procedure outlined.

Objection	Answer
1. _____	_____
2. _____	_____
3. _____	_____
4. _____	_____
5. _____	_____

PROCESS STEP NO. 7: THE DELIVERY

He who has done his best for his own time has lived for all times.
∽ JOHANN VON SCHILLER

All of the effort you've put into the first six steps of the sales process can be wiped out during the delivery step, if performed incorrectly. Many salespeople take this step for granted. They believe that since their client now has or is using the product or service, they'll remain loyal. That's not true. This new client isn't loyal yet; loyalty comes from what you'll be doing in the follow-up step, but it begins in the delivery process.

Delivering your product or service develops the showperson in you. The adrenaline of making the sale has been diminished. Salespeople love the rush of the sale, and as soon as the sale is complete they want to move on to the next one. But make sure you slow down. You still have your delivery.

A delivery takes many forms, especially when you're delivering an intangible service, but you need to realize that the apex of the presentation for you was when your prospect said "yes" and became your client. The height of the sales presentation for your prospect is when your product or service is delivered.

Because of the difference in the timing of the excitement for each of you during the presentation, it's imperative that your showmanship increase. Any hint that the delivery is a necessary evil to your new client reduces all the trust and relationship building that you've developed up to this point.

To build on this excitement and the showmanship that you're using, your delivery must be conducted with perfection. Make a decision to choreograph your delivery process. This means deciding exactly how this presentation will be made to your new client. Remember your client is excited at this point and may also need reassurance. Now is the time to build on both emotions.

Each step of this process must be practiced to perfection. When a top automobile salesperson delivers a new vehicle to the new buyer, they begin by going over the features and the accompanying functions. Top automotive salespeople may:
- Keep cleaning solution and a rag to wipe down smudges on the vehicle
- Wear white gloves to keep their fingerprints off of the new vehicle
- Show but let the clients make their own personalized adjustments on features such as the radio
- Open everything that has a hinge, so after everything is closed, the delivery is complete

If your delivery has a number of areas to cover, such as a new vehicle delivery, you may also want to develop a checklist to make sure you've covered everything. Have your client sign the checklist and give them a copy. This adds to your credibility, honesty and professionalism. Your client sees this as a way to continue the trust relationship you've developed.

What about taking a picture of your new client at delivery with their new purchase? Remember that one of the reasons you're performing an effective delivery is to reinforce and reassure that purchasing your product/service was the right thing to do. By having a picture taken of your new client with their product, you're adding to the showmanship of your delivery.

After the delivery, send a copy of the picture to your client's home or office that has been laminated with your business card and has a small magnet attached. When was the last time anyone threw away a picture of himself or herself?

Many people put this picture in a prominent location for display, such as the refrigerator at home. At the office, the picture is generally near their desk. Not only does this picture reinforce their decision to purchase from you, but it also gives your new client the opportunity to show off the product and to give your phone number to their friends!

There's as much risk in doing nothing as in doing something.

ov TRAMMEL CROW

Action No. 1: If your delivery involves a number of items or areas to cover, develop a checklist to make sure you've covered everything while you're with your client. Make a copy and give it to your client.

Action No. 2: Write down a few ways that you can incorporate showmanship into your delivery. Begin to use them at your earliest opportunity.

1. _____

_____

2. _____

_____

3. _____

_____

4. _____

_____

5. _____

_____

PROCESS STEP NO. 8: THE NEW PROSPECT – GETTING REFERRALS

According to a study by "Behavioral Sciences Research Press" in Dallas, Texas, some 80% of all new salespeople who fail within their first year do so because of insufficient prospecting activity. ("Selling" January/February 1994)

The most difficult and painful step in the sales process for many salespeople is prospecting and most importantly, getting referrals. Not only is the act of prospecting a painful process, but many salespeople have no idea what prospecting truly is or have ever been trained to develop a prospecting system. Most salespeople fail early in their career because of an inability to understand how to receive names of individuals or companies that will do business with them.

The prospecting methods below were able to help me produce approximately 400 prospects per month. As a result, my biggest problem was not in getting the names but having the time to sell everyone! Since this was an impossibility, I was qualifying every new prospect and spending my time handling only those that were Class "A." We'll discuss classes of prospects next, but class "A" prospects are the ones most likely to buy. This is why my negotiation average was near 80 percent and I was the top salesperson for the company I worked for seven years in a row. What worked for me will work for you!

Using any three of the following prospecting methods will continually fill your prospecting pipeline and keep money flowing forever.

Referrals

First, you need to understand exactly what a prospect is not. A prospect is not a name out of a phone book. A prospect is not a person walking into your establishment or calling you on the phone for more information. These are suspects. There's nothing wrong with having a large number of suspects, but these are not individuals you have any control over, nor can you project any future business.

A prospect is an individual or business that:
  a) Has been referred to you by someone with influence
  b) Has the money to buy
  c) Has the need of or wants your product or service

This is called a class A prospect. If one of the above is missing, you usually have a class B prospect. And if two of the three are missing, it's a class C prospect, or a suspect.

What are A, B, and C prospects? B and C are usually easy to understand. But what is meant by "referred by someone with influence"? This individual with influence is important enough that when their name is dropped to the prospect, you at least have their full attention. This doesn't have to be someone important or famous. It can simply be someone who knows the prospect well enough that they trust you initially because you know the individual that has the influence.

Now that you understand what a prospect is, it's a matter of understanding who you want your prospect to be. Very few businesses can sell to everyone, or even if they could, they would need to develop a specific focus so that a majority of their business would be to that specific segment of the population. The first step is to either decide who you want your prospect to be or go through your past records and develop a psychograph of your past clientele.

Develop key demographic characteristics of important elements of your prospect, such as:
  Sex
  Age
  Zip code
  Profession
  Income, etc.

Once you have the preferred qualities of your prospect, go through the sales you've made for the last six months to a year and see who primarily buys your product or service. This should give you an indication of who will probably buy in the future. Instead of a shotgun approach to sell everyone, you narrow your focus toward those who already have an inclination to buy.

If you are going to develop this characteristic list from scratch, decide what kind of prospect you'd like to be selling. Again, if you don't make the decisions about these potential clients that you want to sell to, someone else probably will . . . your prospects! This also goes for those who already have been selling. If you're not happy with the demographics of the buyers you're selling to, change your buyer!

The next step is to develop an objective for the number of new prospects you want to fill the pipeline with on a regular basis (you set this number in Part Two - #11 CCDA). This objective should be set daily, weekly and monthly and strictly adhered to. This is the lifeblood of your future business and career. My suggestion is to decide the number of new leads you need based on the business you are currently doing and increase the number slightly to make you work to achieve the new results.

Achieve your result daily! To accomplish this, develop a list of five questions based on the demographics you developed earlier. These five questions will be asked of everyone you run into on a daily basis. By asking everyone you meet, you'll achieve your result.

But this is where many salespeople get bogged down. They say they've asked their clients for referrals and haven't received any. It's not the fact that your clients don't want to help, it's the way you go about asking the question.

For instance, when you ask, "do you know anyone else who would be interested in our product or service today?" you are causing your client to work too hard. In most cases, he/she can't think of anybody who's interested now. Instead of asking for them to decide who is a buyer now, ask them questions about people they know who fit your demographic profile.

Let's go back to those questions again. Develop those five questions based on the same criteria we developed before. The questions would be similar to these:

1) Who do you know who owns their own business?

2) Who do you know who earns over $100,000 each year?

3) Who do you know who manages people?

4) Who do you know who's especially interested in developing their people?

5) Who do you know who lives in . . . ?

As you ask your client these questions, you can also ask subquestions in the same category. For instance, after the first question above, you can ask:

a) Who do you know who owns a manufacturing business?

b) Who do you know who wants to start a business?

c) Who do you know who has been in business over ten years?

d) Who do you know who has more than one location?

e) Who do you know who owns a franchise?

These questions will be easy for your client to answer because you're not asking him/her to make a decision whether the prospect will buy. You're simply asking for an introduction. Now you have at least from twenty-five to thirty questions to ask everyone you run into. Your confidence will run so high that you'll always achieve your results.

Many salespeople believe the only good referrals come from those who buy. It's actually the opposite. Many prospects feel bad when they don't buy and they want to help. Even though they haven't bought from you, these individuals have a need to do something for you. Use this to your advantage. Guilt is a wonderful thing.

Since you have an objective to receive names of individuals, what happens when you don't hit your objective? You go to the other five methods (to be discussed below) and use two of them as your daily backup. Remember that 60 percent of your prospecting time should be spent finding the ideal prospect you defined earlier.

Whatever you do, plant the referral seed early. Ask your prospect if they mention names of individuals during the interview. Mention to your prospect early during your presentation that they may know other individuals or companies that may have interest in your product or service. And always offer to give your prospect a referral first. This is a great way to "prime the referral pump!"

Action: Begin to develop the questions needed to receive your referral objective. Your referral objective should have been decided in Part II. Now let's develop the questions necessary to elicit the names from your clients. Write out five broad questions and five additional secondary questions that will cause your client to "introduce" you to new referrals.

Major Questions:

1. _____

_____

2. _____

_____

3. _____

_____

4. _____

_____

5. _____

_____

Secondary Questions:

1. _____

_____

2. _____

_____

3. _____

_____

4. _____

_____

5. _____

_____

Centers of Influence

Referrals should always be your number one source to feed your prospect box. But in addition to receiving referrals, you need to cultivate a number of your clients and make them your centers of influence.

A center of influence is an individual who is continually on the lookout for individuals to send to you. These centers of influence care about you and your business. Treat these individuals like gold, because they are. The prospects they introduce you to buy, not just because of you and your product/service, but because they trust the center of influence. Your center of influence will always be on the lookout for prospects. You can then pick up the phone, call your prospect and you'll make your next sale.

So where do you find these centers of influence? They're all around you. These are your clients (and sometimes these are individuals who have never done business with you, but they want to help) who have given you names of prospects who have bought and bought rather easily from the referrer. Determine the number of centers of influence you would like to have and then watch how prospects respond to the referrer. If an immediate trust develops because of the referrer and their "lid" comes down quickly, this is a person you want to cultivate.

You do this by getting to know this individual as best you can. Not only are you receiving names from your center of influence but you're also doing things for them. Remember that you're not buying names from them. You're simply reciprocating because of the help that they've given you.

Action: Who are your potential centers of influence. Write down five names of individuals who could fit these criteria and whom you will develop into strong centers of influence:

1. _____

_____

2. _____

_____

_____

3. _____

_____

4. _____

_____

5. _____

_____

Speaking Engagements

What better way to get in front of potential clients in a nonthreatening situation than in a low-key speaking engagement! Here, you have the opportunity to talk about your product or service, and more importantly, your prospects have a chance to begin to develop trust and confidence in you.

Speaking engagements allow your "suspects" to see you "in action." Your talk allows these individuals to judge you on what they see and hear. Interestingly, it's not what you actually say that they're judging but rather your sincerity about your subject.

So where do you find these speaking engagements? They're all around you! First of all, decide who your class A prospect is (refer to the last section). Next, find all the clubs and organizations that these prospects belong to. Examples include:

Lion's clubs

Ambucs (American Business Clubs)

ABWA (American Business Women's Association)

Rotary

Chambers of Commerce

Call your local Chamber of Commerce to receive a list of these organizations with the phone number of the program chairperson. These individuals are searching for speakers since their organization meets every week (and good speakers are very hard to find). Most would jump at the chance to have you speak.

Next, prepare your talk. Most such organizations let speakers have around twenty minutes. Make your talk an interesting generic discussion about whatever business you're in. For example, here are a few professions with subject titles:

Automobile sales – "How to buy a new car."

"What women should do before buying a new vehicle."
Copier sales – "How to save money using office machinery."
Real Estate sales – "How to Sell Property Fast!"
"How to make your listing attract buyers."

These are just a few examples. But make sure whatever you do, you don't make this a twenty-minute commercial! As a matter of fact, the less you talk about yourself and your company, the more your audience trusts and believes in you. As a result, your audience sees you as an expert in your field. And experts make sales to these individuals.

Now, how do you get these individuals to raise their hands as prospective clients? Have a prize drawing at the end of your talk for a product or service from your company. We're talking about something probably between $10 and $15. Here are a few examples:

Cassette tape with generic information about your topic
Promotional items with your company name (caps, T-shirts, etc.)
Discounts from your firm or others
Free items from your company

But here's where I've had a tremendous amount of success with this process. Before the members turn in their business cards, have them turn their cards over and write "yes, I have interest in finding out more about your business," or "no, I have no interest." I've told the audience that if they leave the card blank I'd consider that a "yes." That's one way to make sure every card has a "yes" or "no." If you have a client in this organization, have them stand up and give a testimonial about doing business with you before they put "yes" or "no."

Most of these people will think you'll send them information. Actually, you'll call everyone that put a "yes" on his or her card. In my early days in the self-development field, I received approximately 75 percent "yes" responses, with about half buying or more than one third of the organization becoming a client of mine!

This works because your prospect has seen you and has interest in what you had to say. Next, they basically said, "Please call me and show me how your product/service will do the things you've talked about."

Between referrals and speaking engagements, you should receive more prospects than you can handle. Actually, what better problem could you have!

Action: Which organizations are you aware of that you'd like to speak to? Write down the names of these organizations that have members similar to your class A prospect. Get the phone numbers from the white pages of your phone book or from your local Chamber of Commerce:

Organization	Phone Number
1. _____	_____
2. _____	_____
3. _____	_____
4. _____	_____
5. _____	_____

Direct Mail

Direct mail can become one of your top sources for receiving prospects. Many companies swear by direct mail; others absolutely swear at it! I'd like to suggest a planned approach to making direct mail effective.

First of all, as we've done in each section, decide who your class A prospect is. Once that's completed, it will be much easier for you to decide whom to put on your mailing list. There is any number of ways to get mailing lists. One is to purchase the list from a list broker. There are located in your local yellow pages. But why spend money with list brokers when you can develop these ideal lists on your own?

Since you know whom you want your client to be, it's now a matter of finding what lists your future client is on. One of the great bank robbers of all time said when asked why he robbed banks,

---

Because that's where the money is!
ᖆ WILLIE SUTTON

Go where your clients are! Whenever you meet with a prospect and you ask your five magic questions, make sure one of these questions is "Are you a member of any groups or organizations?" Since the person you're calling on is a class A prospect, he/she probably associates with other class A prospects. "Birds of a feather flock together!"

Your next two questions will be "Do you have a list of all the members?" And, "May I make a copy?" Should they give you their list, what you now have is a referral list of prospects that you actually could call for meetings. But rather than call every one of them, have them raise their hands for more information.

Instead of developing a mailing that you immediately send out to everyone on the list, send only the number of mailings that you can follow up over the next three to five days. Some of these prospects will contact you (see below) but most won't, even though they have the interest. (Most direct mailings return less than two to three percent, which means over 95 percent of your potential clients should be contacted by phone. These are the ones who don't return your mailing.)

If you mail out more than you can handle by phone, you'll be wasting precious leads that can turn into sales. If it takes too long to get back to these individuals, they'll have forgotten about the mailing. It may take a few mailings to decide how many you should mail.

Your mailing doesn't have to be elaborate, but it must be effective. Make the prospect want to call or respond by offering something if they do. It's best to tie this offer into whatever you're selling, but do make it something that is of some value and/or interest to your prospect. Items such as the ones described in the "speaking engagements" section may work well.

Here's your script for contacting individuals who have responded to your offer:

"John, this is Sam Stone with ABC Technologies. Do you have a moment? You recently responded to our offer of a _____. I'm calling to set a time to get this to you. May I ask a question first? What motivated you to want the _____?"

A couple of things are happening here. First, you've connected with your prospect by letting them know they'll receive their gift. Second, you're finding out what their level of interest is by asking about what motivated them to respond. Once you know you have a true prospect and you have the answer to their questions, set the meeting using the script from Process Step No. 1.

Remember, if a suspect doesn't answer the question correctly (in other words you don't feel they are a true class A prospect) you don't have to waste your time or their time. Simply mail the gift to them and finish the conversation by asking, "Who do you know . . ."

You'll also want to contact all of the nonresponders. This will be a much larger group than the responders, since at best you'll receive five percent of your mailing.

The reason for calling all of the nonresponders is that they may be better prospects than those that did respond. Research has shown that one reason people do not respond to offers is that they have a hard time saying no and/or know they may have a difficult time not buying. By contacting everyone you mail to, you may be able increase your success with this list one hundred fold!

Your script would be similar to this:

"John, this is Sam Stone of ABC Technologies. Do you have a moment? You recently received a mailing from us for a free _____. I'm calling to set a time to get together with you and give you your _____. Which is better for you, Monday at 10 A.M. or Tuesday at 1 P.M.?"

If you receive any objections or questions, use the cold call script from Process Step No. 1.

Action No.1: Where will you find your lists? Make a list of five individuals who are members of organizations who will help you by making a copy of their membership roster.

1. _____

   _____

2. _____

   _____

3. _____

   _____

4. _____

   _____

5. _____

   _____

Action No. 2: What will you say to your responders and nonresponders? Pull out the script you developed from Process Step No. 1 and write out your direct mail script.

Cold Calling

Cold calling has been saved for last since it's the one prospecting source that salespeople say they hate, yet most salespeople tend to use as their last resort. Cold calling doesn't have to be as painful as most salespeople make it, yet it can provide a significant source of prospects. Cold calls can also reach individuals and businesses that you wouldn't normally sell to. But you must understand how to use cold calling correctly.

A couple of should nots: Cold calling shouldn't be used as a substitute for any of the other methods already discussed. Cold calling shouldn't be used as your primary prospecting source.

Instead, cold calling should be used to fill the void where your other methods are leaving holes. For instance, when you're in an office building making a presentation to an individual, call on the company next door. When you've had success with a certain individual or business, contact individuals or businesses that fit a similar description. Cold calling gets you in front of prospects that you may not have received as leads in any other way.

What do you do when you cold call? Your objective is not to make a sales presentation. Instead, you want to qualify the prospect enough so that they will set a meeting with you. For instance, when you're cold calling in person, ask the receptionist who the person is that you're looking for. If that person is not there, hand the receptionist your business card and tell her that you'll be calling this person. This sets you up for the next call.

If the prospect is in, ask to introduce yourself to this person. After exchanging business cards, ask permission to call to discuss setting a time to get together at a later date or ask, "When can I have twenty minutes of your time to introduce myself and my company to you?"

This gives your new prospect a little breathing room, so they can understand that you're not there to just sell but to develop a relationship to possibly sell later. When you call, remind your prospect of your first meeting and continue setting up the meeting. Now cold calling has become warm calling, and you're playing the odds in your favor. Their "lid" has come down and you're beginning to "see the whites of their eyes!"

A variation of the cold call process is observation. How many individuals and/or businesses do you pass by on any single day? They're all potential prospects! Make a list of these businesses and organizations that would make ideal clients.

I sold radio advertising a number of years ago and used this method as my primary source of new leads. One of my first sales positions was in a small town in the Midwest. Since I was one of five salespeople, and since the other four had been there much longer than I had, I needed to find a new source of business. I joined the local Chamber of Commerce and became active in the Ambassadors Club. This group goes by a number of names, but their primary purpose is to sell memberships into the Chamber of Commerce.

I became extremely adept at observing. Anytime I saw that a new business might come into the area, I would immediately contact the company and sell a membership. I was getting my foot in the door before I presented any radio advertising. Interestingly, almost every company I sold a membership to also became a client on the radio station I represented.

This process is part of the trust and relationship building. By getting to know me in a nonthreatening sales situation, my client felt more comfortable dealing with me, and the relationship was established. The last year I spent in that town I sold more chamber memberships than anyone in towns with a population less than fifty thousand. The running gag from the competing radio stations was that I knew that companies were coming to town before the business did!

Action No. 1: Which companies have you been driving by that need your product or service? Now's the time to strike! Write them down!

1. _____

2. _____

3. _____

4. _____

5. _____

Action No. 2: Success in cold calling is the direct result of determining the number of cold calls you'll make per week and sticking to it. My suggestion is to make one cold call per day, just after your last call of the day. Call on the business next door or near the business you're already calling on. What's your objective for cold calls each week?

Objective: _____

When will you make these cold calls? _____

What will you say when you cold call a suspect?

Eight Additional Successful Prospecting Methods

There are numerous additional methods of getting names of individuals and/or companies to call on. You're only limited by your own imagination.

Additional Cold Calls:

1) One successful method for finding decision makers is to check local job books that have the names of the human resources directors. These individuals hold the purse strings for a tremendous number of projects.

2) The phone book is always a great source. But remember to begin your calls at the end of the phone book rather than at the beginning. Most every salesperson begins by calling the As, and they quit somewhere in the middle of the alphabet (if they get that far). These individuals and companies have figured out how to handle salespeople long ago since they receive so many calls. It's the X, Y and Zs that have no idea what to do with you since they never receive any calls!

3) During my time selling advertising, I used the old standbys for getting names—mainly media such as radio, TV, the newspaper, yellow pages and billboards. Where should you go to receive names of individuals or companies to call? You go where your clients are.

Friends: Another overlooked method of receiving excellent leads is through your friends. They can be one of your best sources since they're constantly on the look-out for individuals and/or companies that may buy from you.

By developing your friends as "prospect hunters," you broaden your range of people and companies to turn into prospects. Your friends become your additional eyes and ears to find the right kind of prospect for you.

You've developed your friends over the years, and true friends want to continually help each other. Would you do whatever it took to help your friends? Use, but don't abuse, this relationship to help each other. Remember to be on the lookout for prospects for your friends, too.

Salespeople: Another area that has tremendous nuggets to "mine" is other salespeople. Get together regularly with non-competitive salespeople. You can do this on your own, form a group, or find other networking groups to join and work within. The downside to memberships in networking groups is that you don't get a chance to know everyone well, and therefore many members may be reluctant to share names of prospective clients. The upside is that you may regularly receive a large number of names.

My suggestion is to network with other salespeople individually on a regular basis. You get to know each other better and are more likely to share names with someone you trust. Make sure that these salespeople are with industries that complement or work with the industry you represent.

Previous Clients: One of the most overlooked areas for doing additional business is a client you've already done business with. All it takes is a phone call. The worst that will happen is they have no interest in doing business with you again. But they can always supply you with a number of referrals or introductions!

Orphan Clients: While you're contacting past clients, why not check to see what other clients salespeople who are no longer with your company have not called on recently. Because of turnover within sales forces, many companies call these "orphan" clients since their salesperson left the company, and they've become "orphaned." These clients might not have purchased recently because either they couldn't work with the last salesperson or more than likely, that last salesperson never put the effort into following up and developing this client.

Reestablish rapport with these "orphaned" clients, sell them and their referrals. They bought from your company before and they may buy again and bring their friends and associates with them!

Business Contacts: You should never forget companies and people you already spend money with. They may not necessarily do anymore business with you, but because you're already doing business with them, they're more than likely to at least sit down with you and discuss your business. Again, at worst, they won't buy from

you but this is an excellent opportunity for these individuals to become great centers of influence and send class A prospects to you on a regular basis.

Whatever you do, use three of the above methods as your primary source of leads and let cold calling fill in your gaps.

I'd rather be a master prospector than a wizard
of speech with no one to tell my story to.
∾ PAUL J. MEYER, SMI

Action: Why don't sales consultants receive as many referrals as they would like? They don't ask. Why don't they ask? Because their clients say that when they think of someone, they'll let them know. They never do. So there's no reason asking since they never receive any referrals.

The problem isn't that sales consultants don't ask. The problem is they ask the wrong questions at the wrong times.

1. Write down your objective for the number of referrals that you would like to receive from each client from Part II of this book.

   _____

2. Set an objective for the number of referrals you would like to receive every day, each week and each month.

   _____

   Number of new leads/day, week or month: _____

   Number of referrals from each client: _____

3. Decide which three prospecting methods (from the preceding page) you'll use daily. Preferably using referrals as your first method:
   a) Referrals

   b) _____

   c) _____

4. Do it every day

PROCESS STEP NO. 9: THE FOLLOW-UP–RELATIONSHIP MANAGEMENT

We have two ears and one tongue in order that
we may hear more and speak less.

∾ DIOGENES

Now the process begins all over again. Remember that once a client buys, they become a prospect for another sale. Most salespeople don't take the time, effort, or money to ever thank their clients. Does this mean they'll lose their business? They probably won't, but why take the chance? To keep your client buying, there are methods to continue this relationship. The first method is through etiquette.

Our grandparents' lives focused on etiquette. Today courtesy hasn't disappeared, but it also hasn't been emphasized quite as much as it use to be. Since being polite isn't in vogue, those salespeople who treat their clients well are unique.

Thank You: What do we mean by being polite? Asking permission and saying thank you is very important. We discussed asking permission with the "prospect agreement." Let's discuss saying thank you. Recall the last time someone you bought from sent you a thank-you card or phoned to thank you. I'll bet at best you've received one card, at worst, you've never been thanked. As a result, those individuals who send a card or make a call in order to thank clients stand out as unique.

If you want your clients talking about you, wouldn't you want them to remember that you sent them a thank-you card to show you care? A thank-you can also be more than just thanking a client for their business. It can also be a birthday or holiday card. As we get older, we begin to receive fewer birthday cards. So the few cards we receive begin to stand out. One major car rental company sends me a birthday card each year with a certificate to add 500 airline miles toward any airline I want. Do you think I consider them when I'm planning on renting a car? You bet!

Newsletter: As a salesperson, you want to be remembered. One of the best ways is to keep your name in front of your clients on a regular basis. A great way to do that while selling yourself and your ideas is to send a quarterly newsletter.

This newsletter can serve as an in-depth calling card and a way to let your clients know more about you and more about what you're selling. The quarterly newsletter I send won't win any creativity prizes, but my clients and potential clients do mention it when I call. Included on the newsletter are all of the phone numbers and addresses to contact me, including my Web site (more about that below).

How many of your competitors have a newsletter? That's what I thought, probably very few, if any. How are you going to look to your clients and prospects when they begin to receive information from you on a regular basis? Doing business today comes down to whom a client can trust and a person they can remember. As mentioned before, when I sold advertising, it was referred to as a USP, "unique selling proposition."

Whatever you're selling, you want your clients and prospects to see you as unique and different. Your newsletter can do this for you.

Web site: How about your own Web site? Not only are you selling your company, but also you're selling yourself. Your Web site can provide a lot of information for your clients without their having to contact you. You can also link your site to your company's site so that your client can always stay in touch with you.

One basic premise to remember is that your client wants you to stay in touch with them, because it makes them feel that you care. It doesn't matter what methods you use; your client just wants to know that whenever they need you, you'll be there. Remember that you're the safety net for your client and a major part of what they paid for was service after the sale. This service means that you should be available to deal with whatever problems or needs your client may have.

And here's another benefit from developing the follow-up habit: additional business from those prospects who just don't buy right away. I have a number of clients who have done business with me after I followed up with them over months and years. The same premise is in place: that when these prospects, just like your clients, are ready to buy, they buy from that source who they're most comfortable with. You've followed up with them; therefore you're the most natural source to do business with.

Gifts: Don't forget gifts to your clients. There are many occasions when you could give gifts. For example:
1. As a thank-you for a prospect who becomes a new client
2. For their continued business
3. If your client makes an unusually large purchase

If you keep your clients in mind and know as much as you can about them, purchasing gifts is very easy.

Why purchase gifts for clients? Not only do clients like being thanked for their business, but they also like to know that they are special to you as their salesperson.

Gifts can help make that situation special. We're not talking about expensive presents but about gifts that tell your client "you're special."

Gift ideas:
    Tickets to ballgames, movies, and the theatre
    Gift certificates
    Books
    Video/cassette tapes
    T-shirts/caps (with your logo)

By the way, if you're giving two tickets to a client, buy four and go with them. Whatever money you spend will come back to you quickly by the additional friendship and relationship building developed during this outing. Again we're not talking about buying your client's trust; we're talking about thanking your client.

What should the gift cost? The cost should be commensurate to the amount of business your client has been giving to you. Sometimes, the smaller, but more thoughtful, the better. Holiday presents should also fit within this category. Send something thoughtful. But be sensitive to cultural and religious beliefs. The wrong gift could backfire!

The types of gifts I prefer to send fit inside an envelope. There's no wrapping and no additional shipping expense. Also, your client has no idea they're receiving a present until they open the envelope. Items that work well include:
    Long distance telephone cards
    Video rental cards
    $1,000,000 bills

The last one is a little different. These bills are printed on the same quality paper used by the US Mint. They actually look like real money! What better way to say, "Thanks a million!" In addition, none of the gifts have my name or company name printed anywhere on it. There's a reason for this. Printed items are mass-produced and can be given to anyone. They're designed to promote you and your business.

Nonprinted items seem more individualized and personal. As a matter of fact, your client won't forget whom they received that million-dollar bill from and every time they see it they think of you. Just use your imagination and give something clever and inexpensive. You just want them to think about you, not buy their business. Each of the items above is in the ten-dollar range, not enough to offend but just enough to remember.

Paralyze their resistance with your persistence.

ભ WOODY HAYES

Action No. 1: What do you do to follow-up? What kind of system do you have in place to effectively follow-up? Indicate below the follow-up techniques that you will use to set yourself apart from all the other salespeople who either do not follow-up or make only a minor attempt. Be creative! Write down the ideas you'll start using:

1. _____

2. _____

3. _____

4. _____

5. _____

Action No. 2: How can you thank your clients? Make a list of the clients you have that either are centers of influence and/or are your best clients. Next, develop a list of gifts that are relatively inexpensive but show that you appreciate their business and help.

Clients

1. _____

2. _____

3. _____

4. _____

5. _____

Gift Ideas

1. _____

2. _____

3. _____

4. _____

5. _____

Repetition Through Persistence

Whoever perseveres will be crowned.
ﻬ JOHANN HERDER

One thing you can always depend on for success in the sales game is persistence through repetition. Not giving up will guarantee you a certain degree of success. When confronted with obstacles, most people give up. Quitting is a guarantee of failure. Simply beginning and not stopping gives you success.

Here's an example of sticking with it: Two frogs fell into separate pails of milk. One frog swam and swam, getting tired and thinking that there was probably nothing he could do to get out of the pail. So he quit swimming, sunk to the bottom and drowned.

The other frog kept swimming, though tired, realized that if he swam long enough, he could turn the milk into butter, which he did and he hopped out. That's persistence! And the persistence occurred through repetition.

Great people are ordinary people with extraordinary amounts of determination.
ﻬ AUTHOR UNKNOWN

As with the first frog, nothing ever happens without persistence through repetition. We need to persist, whether something has worked or not. Most people give up after the first exposure. You are going to skin your knees, and you are going to hurt, but if you don't stick to it, you're not going to grow. Growth begins with persistence.

The height that great men reached and kept were not obtained by sudden flight,
but while their companions slept were toiling upward into the night!
ﻬ HENRY WADSWORTH LONGFELLOW

It takes a tremendous amount of patience to develop determination and persistence. Successful people develop the habit of patience and persistence.

Have you ever wondered how the Grand Canyon was formed? Was it from something hitting the earth with such force that it carved a hole that deep and that long? Or was it the Colorado River that, over the years, simply carved a canyon so deep that people from far and wide admire its immensity? Repetition created the Grand Canyon. Repetition can help to create any objective in your life also.

You never know when a buyer will want your product or service. Why is it that direct marketers continue sending the same advertisement to you endlessly? Why do you see the same commercials over and over on television? Advertisers realize that it takes a concept called "spaced repetition" to sell the majority of buyers. Sixty-two percent of everything you know has been presented to you at least six times. In school we called it "rote learning." In the military it's called "brain washing." Whatever name it goes by, this is how we learn.

Can you tell what companies used the following slogans?
  a) "Where's the beef?"
  b) " . . . Tastes good like a cigarette should."
  c) "Two all beef patties . . . "
  d) "You'll wonder where the yellow went . . . "

For those of you who are too young or were snoozing:
  a) Wendy's
  b) Winston
  c) McDonald's
  d) Pepsodent

Can you still repeat the alphabet, even though it's been years since you recited it? What's 9 x 9? All right, what's 19 x 19? It wasn't as easy was it? The reason we know 9 x 9 = 81 is because we learned certain multiplication tables through rote learning. The reason that you didn't automatically know that 19 x 19 = 361 was because you never went that far through the multiplication tables.

But we can learn most anything if we simply go over the information continually until it becomes a part of us. It's the same for your prospects. The more you call on them, the more they see your face and hear your name; and the more you remind them of how important your product or service is to them, the more likely they will become your client.

How many products do you buy simply because you've seen so much advertising that the product or service has become familiar to you? Because of habits, we tend to focus on those things that are most familiar to us, those things that are on our minds. Our mind is a mental magnet, which attracts what we think about all day. We remember the things we say, think or do and that which is put in front of us on a daily basis.

To keep your clients focused on you, it's imperative that you keep focused on them by repetition. Be persistent but not overwhelming in contacting them. Telephoning is good since that's your primary method of staying in touch with your clients and/or setting meetings. But why not fax your clients once in a while with some new information?

How about an E-mail update about new products or services? Maybe a newsletter to keep your clients informed (more about these in Part Three). These methods are great for additional updates, along with letters. We're not talking about continually sending messages. We're talking about marketing in addition to selling; keeping your name in front of them so that when they're ready to buy they only think about you.

Since your clients buy from those individuals they are most comfortable with, you are now in the driver's seat. Much of this is psychological. Your client may not even know why they prefer you and your product/service to others.

Stick with it! A young jockey once lost his first 250 races. Eddie Arcaro went on to become one of the greatest jockeys ever and won the most money in 1948, 1950, 1952 and 1955. Are you as persistent as Eddie was?

Nothing in the world can take the place of persistence. Talent will not; nothing is more common than unsuccessful men with talent. Genius will not; unrewarded genius is almost a proverb. Education will not; the world is full of educated derelicts. Persistence and determination alone are omnipotent.

∾ CALVIN COOLIDGE

Action: How can you use repetition to make sure your client knows that you care. Write down a few ideas that you plan to do to keep your clients informed:

1. _____

_____

2. _____

_____

3. _____

_____

4. _____

_____

5. _____

_____

The Follow-Up System

"Slump" - *when you've reached a point that the things you don't like to do have become more important than your reasons for doing them.*

∽ AUTHOR UNKNOWN

I remember high school as a time of frustration since I had a hard time fitting everything in. And because I didn't understand basic self-management, I kept running around in circles, never accomplishing what needed to be done. As a result, my study habits weren't great, and I received poor grades.

I finally began to understand self-management during the first semester of my senior year in college when I decided to take extra hours to make my last semester easier so that I could have time to find a job. I hadn't counted on taking all journalism and English courses, with required essays and stories, most with as many as two drafts and a final version.

It was at this point in my life that I realized money was relatively important. While working two jobs, it also became clear that time management was important to accomplish my financial objectives

Where do you begin? First of all, you need a well-developed system to organize all of the names of prospects and clients. The system described below can be accessed anywhere at any time. I've been using this system for over twenty years, and my clients are continually amazed at how well I remember when to follow-up with them. The system is simple. There's no thought involved, as long as you use the system every day.

1) Buy the following supplies (can be bought from any office supply store for under $20):
    a) 3x5 organizer box (looks like a shoebox with a spring-loaded sizer)
    b) 1,000 3x5 cards
    c) A–Z tabs
    d) 1–31 tabs
    e) January–December tabs
    f) Blank tabs: A, B and C
2) Set-up your box. Put the A, B and C tabs in first followed by the "rotating" section, which includes: January–December tabs; next, put in

the 1–31 tabs and finally the A–Z tabs. Each of the 3x5 cards will be used for your prospects and clients.

3) Information to put on the cards includes the following:
   a) Name
   b) Company
   c) Phone: Business/Home/Fax/Pager
   d) Address: Business/Home
   e) E–mail Address: Business/Home
   f) Position
   g) Spouse/Children's Names
   h) Income
   i) Date you received the name
   j) Referred by

(You may even want to have these cards preprinted with the above information. The advantage: not having to remember what information you need to ask for.)

4) As you receive a new referral, put the card behind the A, B or C tabs based on the information you've received from the referrer:
   a) Class A: Referred by someone with influence, has the money to buy and has the need or want
   b) Class B: May be missing some of the above information
   c) Class C: Name and basic information only.

5) Begin calling the class A cards until you run out, then the class B and finally class C. Continually attempt to upgrade the class B and C cards by getting more information about them from friends or the referrer.

6) Once the card is removed from the class A, B or C file, it goes into the rotating section, which includes the remaining tabs.
   a) Let's say this is the month of March, you call your prospect, and a meeting is set for March 23. Put the card behind the tab for 23 since it's the current month. When March 23 rolls around, simply take the card out from behind the slot and meet with your prospect at the time you wrote in your planner.
   b) Maybe you call a prospect and you can't see them until July 10, but today is June 23. Put the card behind the July tab, make a note of the day and when July rolls around take all of the cards behind that tab and put them behind the appropriate days in the 1–31 tabs.
   c) The same goes for any callback or follow up. Simply put the card behind the daily or monthly tab to follow up with.
   d) You continually move your prospect through the system until they buy;

die, or you feel there's no hope of ever selling this individual or company.

e) Once your prospect buys, put together a second card and put it into the A–Z section, which represents your "sold" clients. Here, you'll always be able to find their information without having to hunt for it throughout your system (Suggestion: use a different color card to differentiate sold and unsold).

f) The original card continues within the rotating section, since you will continue to follow up and possibly sell this client again.

7) Most importantly, you must use this system every day. It will work if you work the system. The day you don't use the system is the day the system stops working. (SUCCESS MOTIVATION INSTITUTE, WACO, TX)

There are risks and costs to a program of action, but they are far less than the long-range costs of comfortable inaction.

∞ JOHN F. KENNEDY

Action: Buy the above materials today, and begin a follow-up system that will immediately increase sales and ensure your future success.

a) What does your class A or ideal prospect look like?

1) Occupation/Position _____

2) Industry   _____

3) Age   _____

4) Education _____

5) Income/Financial Status   _____

6) Family Status   _____

7) Hobbies_____

8) Church _____

9) Other   _____

SALES NO. 1-9

In the fields of observation, chance favors the prepared mind.

∾ LOUIS PASTEUR

As you work your way through this nine-step sales process, you're using the prospect agreement discussed at the beginning of this section. Not only do you need to get agreement from your prospect throughout each step of the process, but also each step of the process is a sale and must be negotiated.

Each of these negotiation steps ends with a question. This is the question that keeps you in control but also lets the prospect make a decision. If asked and phrased correctly, your prospect will give you permission to move to the next step. If performed incorrectly, your prospect may move to the next step with you, but reluctantly and the further you move through the sale process, the more difficulty you'll have in asking the final negotiation questions and receiving referrals. Doubt and suspicion begin to increase. If agreement has not yet been reached at any step, you **must** correct this before proceeding further! Their "lid" is up and you can't "see the whites of their eyes!"

Whenever a sale is made with the approval of your prospect, not only have you received permission to move to the next step, but you've also increased the trust and confidence necessary to make the final sale. And as you move from step to step using the prospect agreement, you've also added that trust and confidence and reduced the suspicion and doubt. You can "see the whites of their eyes!"

Behold the turtle! He makes progress only when he sticks his neck out!

∾ JAMES BRYANT CONANT

Action: Do you see each piece of your sales presentation as an individual sale? Decide today to sell by pieces and not as a whole. By developing your sales approach this way, you'll increase your income and number of clients, while developing additional trust and confidence. Rank which pieces of the nine-step process need a better prospect agreement. Begin to work on the first one today!

1. The Contact: _____

_____

2. The Meeting: _____

_____

3. The Interview: _____

_____

4. The Presentation: _____

_____

5. The Negotiation: _____

_____

6. The Reassurance: _____

_____

7. The Delivery: _____

_____

8. The New Prospect: _____

_____

9. The Follow-Up: _____

_____

SALESPERSON VS. SALES CONSULTANT

Once you start, keep at it. Never give up. Push harder when you have to, relax when you can. If you don't keep going until you're satisfied, you will never know how much you can do. You can do anything. Your strength is equal to your need.

∾ PAUL WILLIAMS FROM "DAS ENERGI"

What do you do for a living? Do you sell or do you advise your clients and help them achieve their objectives? If you do the former, you have to go out and create business every day. If you do the latter, you are continually developing business to make your life and the life of your client easier.

I knew a salesperson who sold automobiles for ten years. You'd expect an individual like that to have a lot of repeat and referral business. But he never followed up and, as a result, kept selling the same number of vehicles every year, and working hard to do it.

He didn't have ten years of experience; he had one year of experience ten times! Imagine what his business would have looked like had he become a sales consultant and developed repeat and referral business from his clients?

My father, who was a top salesperson, told me long ago, "Sell something that is used or needs to be replaced." We can't always sell a tangible, but we are always selling an intangible, ourselves. This is the service you are selling when you sell as a sales consultant.

Having to develop new clients every day is difficult to say the least and tedious at best. Many industries, such as new vehicle sales, have a tremendous amount of new prospects coming to them on a daily basis. These are actually the most difficult to develop into long-range clients who will keep buying only from you.

When you are selling to someone who's come to you and you haven't made any effort to develop that client, the loyalty factor is very low. When you need to find new business every day, you're a salesperson. When you develop your own clients and cultivate them with additional business, you are a sales consultant.

If you want to move into the higher echelon of income earners, you need to become a consultant and work with your clients and make them lifetime loyalists.

Studies from many sales consulting companies have shown that the average salesperson gives up before presentation number five. Sixty percent of all sales are made after the fifth call. Only 12 percent of all salespeople make a fifth call. At the third call, the prospect still has doubt but begins to move toward buying. The average buyer begins buying at presentation number seven. Ninety-four percent of all buyers buy by the fifteenth presentation. How many salespeople do you know who persist that long? Do you?

A survey of a thousand retail merchants revealed one of the most blatant shortcomings of salespeople. It was reported that when a salesman made a call on them for the first time and did not make a sale:

48.2% quit after one call

24.4% quit after two calls

14.7% quit after three calls.

Only one salesman out of eight made as many as four calls, yet these same retailers reported that the great bulk of their buying from a new salesman was not made until after his third call.

Never give up unless the client dies or moves out of town!

ꙮ QUOTE POSTED IN A CLIENT'S OFFICE

Trust is developed over time like love is. The only way your prospect is going to trust you and let their "lid" down will be based on what you do for them and with them over time. Nothing can replace time. As a result, when you attempt to sell a product or service to someone before you've earned their trust (and the right to sell them), they feel like they've been pressured to buy and rightly so. Sometimes, this takes fifteen presentations! It takes time to help your prospect get that "lid" down!

Granted, there are a number of industries where you can make a sale very early in the process. But whether you are able to or not, the only way to develop your client base and to keep them loyal is to continually touch them.

In our high-tech world of the Internet and faceless transactions, the average prospect is spending less and less time with a live individual. As a result, there are fewer and fewer opportunities for these prospects to be touched. Being "touched" is used here in psychological terms rather than physical. Whenever you contact your client, you are touching them. Whenever you follow up with a client, you are touching them. No matter how pervasive the Internet becomes, we all have a need, as clients, to be touched. Those salespeople who are able to accomplish this are the sales consultants who will build a strong client base and develop client loyalty.

These are also the sales consultants who are building trust and confidence in their clients. Since they've developed this trust and confidence with these clients, they also have an opportunity to sell their clients at every touch opportunity. As discussed before, at every touch opportunity a salesperson should sell the client something.

For instance, when you follow-up with a client, sell them on when you should call them back. When you make your first presentation to a prospect, sell them on the next meeting. After you've sold a client, sell them on a referral. Whenever you complete the final sales presentation, negotiate for the sale.

Since touch is such a strong part of the equation, keep touching and following up forever, as long as there's potential business. People do business with people they trust and feel care about them. They don't necessarily do business with the salespeople with the best sales skills. Which is one reason why the activity of staying in touch with clients and prospects is more important than your skill level.

What's exciting about the above statement is that ANYONE can be a number one, high-income earning sales consultant. It just takes having the confidence and doing the right things for your clients.

Men do not fail. They give up trying.

☙ ELIHU ROOT

Action: How persistent have you been? Keep track of five to ten prospects and/or clients over the next few months to see how many calls it takes to make the sale:

Client/Prospect	# of Calls
1. _____	_____
2. _____	_____
3. _____	_____
4. _____	_____
5. _____	_____
6. _____	_____
7. _____	_____
8. _____	_____
9. _____	_____
10. _____	_____

PART FOUR

Conditioning
Change for Results

A CONDITIONING FABLE

*We have all been subjected to conditioning. Many of us refuse to go
beyond the bounds of that conditioning. We walk, talk, dress, behave, learn and
earn within the limits of that conditioning. We have been conditioned by
our parents, brothers and sisters, teachers, counselors, clergy, employers—almost
everyone we have trusted, respected and believed.*

*We have become conditioned to feel bad when we want to be good.
The more we ask for, we have learned, the more will be taken away from us. When
we tried to achieve, to be happy, enthusiastic, successful, we were labeled
troublemakers, rabble-rousers, black sheep. We were told we were weird, different,
unusual. Why? Our friends and associates don't want us to succeed.
The better we look, the worse they look. So they call us names. They tell us to cool
it, not to make waves. They tell us not to want too much.*

*We have been conditioned to make small demands on life, to feel bad
because we're good, to feel guilty when we want more. So when we think about
developing new business our conditioning makes us believe we will fail.
It becomes a self-fulfilling prophecy. We fail because we're unwilling to break the*

conditioning that holds us back. Most of us don't have the courage or guts to walk away from the things that aren't good, to walk away from the people who are holding us back, to get those bad ideas, implanted by years of conditioning, out of our lives.

ᖇ FRANKLIN B. BLOOM CMC, "THE PSYCHOLOGY OF RAINMAKING"
JOURNAL OF MANAGEMENT CONSULTANT, JUNE 1995.

Conditioning is the reason you may be at the level of sales you're at right now. The conditioning we accept becomes a habit. And our habits begin to enslave us.

Do you remember hearing as you grew up, "Don't talk to strangers?" Your parents and teachers said this because as a young child this was meant to help protect you.

But then you grew older. And your parents and teachers never told you to unlearn the value that you had been conditioned to use. You then became a salesperson, eager to go out and conquer the world. But for some reason, you just couldn't hit the level of sales you wanted to accomplish. One reason? You were told, "Don't talk to strangers!" What do you do for a living? You "talk to strangers!"

You're in a constant battle with values that were ingrained in you years ago. These values and your objectives just don't mix if they're in conflict, because your values are much stronger than any objectives you set. Values always win out.

Your environment is sure to influence you to some extent for better or worse but it must get your permission before it takes complete charge.

ᖇ JIM CLARK

A number of years ago, I met a young lady who I had been referred to see regarding a self-development program I was selling. As we discussed where she was in her life and where she wanted to be, she mentioned that she hadn't had a full night's sleep in over three years.

I asked why and she told me that she was separated from her husband, and she wanted a divorce. I asked what was holding up the process. She said that she was raised as a Roman Catholic and that her strict upbringing conditioned her to believe "marriage for life."

She would have to change her objective of getting a divorce or change a deeply conditioned value of "marriage for life." Her internal conflict between her values and objectives was ripping her apart.

As a salesperson, it's imperative to understand what kinds of values are holding you back and moving you ahead. You are conditioned by all that has occurred in your life since you were born. You can't get rid of it. No matter what you do to change, a part of you will always be there.

Since a part of your past is always with you, it's simply a matter of understanding and dealing with it. Your past is a part of you. As you change, realize that you are where you are today because of all the things, good or bad, that have happened in the past. The past is gone; the future is ahead. Even though it's a part of you, focus on what "you" want to become.

I once used the excuse of "I'm this way because of the way I was raised," when things weren't going right. Now I say, "I'm this way because of the way I was raised, and I'm going to use it to make myself better!"

All things are difficult before they are easy.
∽ THOMAS FULLER, 17TH CENTURY ENGLISH MINISTER

Action: What are the values that are holding you back from becoming the person and the salesperson you want to become? This may take some thinking, but list at least five values that you have that you'd like to change.

1. _____

_____

2. _____

_____

3. _____

_____

4. _____

_____

5. _____

_____

COMFORT ZONE

Complacency is one step before failure.
∾ AUTHOR UNKNOWN

Your comfort zone is that feeling you have when everything is going right. When you are outside of your comfort zone without preparing for it, your body reacts in the fight or flight mode: you want to run away from the situation, fight the situation or sometimes a little of both. When you prepare for your new, enlarged comfort zone, you can develop the attitudes, behaviors and skills necessary before you get there. Once you arrive at your larger comfort zone, you are better prepared to accept the change, and you easily move into your new mode.

Have you ever walked into the restroom of the opposite sex unintentionally? What was the *first* action thought that went through your head? You wanted to get out as quickly as possible! This happened because you weren't comfortable. You wanted to do whatever you could to move back into an arena of comfort. And comfort was anywhere outside of that restroom at the moment.

The only way we can grow is to expand our comfort zone. We can't break out of our comfort zone, we're simply expanding what we already have. You can never leave what you are; you're simply adding more to where you are.

So how do we expand our comfort zone? Do what you're afraid to do.

What doesn't kill you makes you stronger.
∾ NIETSCHZE

In most cases, we aren't willing to change because we have to think, and thinking is hard work. That's why we use so little of our conscious mind on a daily basis. Psychology experts have said that at any given time our subconscious part of our mind is active about 90 percent, while our conscious mind is used about 10 percent. Most of what we do daily is automatic and reactionary. We rarely think, we just do. The reason we don't enjoy change is that it makes us think. Change makes us expand our comfort zone. We move into an area that isn't comfortable.

For instance, when you pick up a glass to drink, your subconscious mind is helping you with the activity. On a daily basis, we have more of these types of activities compared to "thinking" or conscious activities. Those who are most successful are those who are continually expanding their comfort zone by doing that which isn't comfortable and focusing on where they'd like to be.

But something interesting begins to happen. As these individuals continue to do what isn't comfortable, this becomes the standard and is now comfortable, and it's done without thinking. As a result, these individuals continue to improve leaps and bounds ahead of everyone else simply because it has now become a natural part of their being.

But the problem with enlarging our comfort zone is that it occurs slowly. Picture your home thermostat. If you want to warm your home from 65 degrees to 75 degrees, you simply turn the thermostat up to 75. But is it now instantly warm? No, because it takes the furnace a while to heat your home to 75. It's the same with us. We need to mentally be at 75 degrees before we're actually at 75 degrees. We need to develop our expanded comfort zone in our heads first before we're actually there.

The mind, once expanded to the dimensions of larger ideas,
never returns to its original size.
∾ OLIVER WENDELL HOLMES

Until you know exactly where you want to be, you can't turn your thermostat to that spot and, as a result, you can't expand your comfort zone since you don't know where you want to expand it.

I had a client a number of years ago who worked for a large corporation and wanted to get into the computer field on straight commission. The year I met him he was making $45,000. His fourth month in his new field he made $40,000, in one month selling computers! You'd think a month like that would cause him to have an exceptional year. He finished the year at $50,000!

What happened? His mind was so locked into his earlier salary of $45,000 (his comfort zone) that once he hit that figure, his subconscious mind shut down. It wasn't that he didn't want to make more money. It was because subconsciously he was only worth $45,000 and his subconscious put the brakes on his earnings once he hit his previous comfort zone.

He worked on enlarging his comfort zone and his attitude by focusing on where he wanted to be and seeing himself at that income. The end of his second year he made $100,000.

You are your comfort zone, and it and your self-image are the same. Your self-image will immediately begin to get larger as your comfort zone expands. You'll see yourself and what you can do in an entirely different light; a light that will shine much farther than it shines right now! Work to enlarge your comfort zone to deal with any conditioning you're not happy with.

Courage is not the absence of fear, it is the conquest of it.
∾ FRANK BETTGER

Action: How will you change the values you previously wrote down? Pick one of the five values you'd like to change and describe how you will go about changing it to enlarge your comfort zone.

Value: _____

Change Plan: _____

_____

_____

HABIT

We are what we repeatedly do. Excellence then is not an act, but a habit.

∽ ARISTOTLE

Habits are the clothing a nun wears. Why? Because habits are comfortable! Your habit is your comfort zone. You stay in your comfort zone because it's comfortable.

But what happens, for example, when you begin to gain or lose weight? All of a sudden your clothes don't fit as well as you'd like them to. As a result, you either tailor your clothes to your new measurements or you purchase new ones.

Your average level of sales activity is your habit. You can change and enlarge this level of activity by putting on a new "sales habit." Enlarging this sales comfort zone and changing sales habits is almost as easy as buying new clothes. It's a matter of knowing what your new, larger comfort zone is going to feel like.

During your clothes shopping, you try on any number of new outfits before you purchase the one that is "you!" You only know which outfit is right for you after you try it on and look at yourself in the mirror.

Your life and personality are largely the product of your daily habits.
You develop precisely in the way in which you exercise your various powers.
Actions repeated long enough become automatic.

∽ GRENVILLE KLEISER

Let's go shopping for your larger "comfort zone." Decide what type of comfort zone and habits you'd like to have and begin to "see" yourself in this larger comfort zone. Look at yourself in your new zone from all angles and change whatever it is about this new picture that isn't right. Just as you won't wear clothes that don't fit, don't wear a new comfort zone that isn't "comfortable."

Many individuals back off from any sudden change that thrusts them into a new situation or comfort zone. They wore those new clothes for a short time and since they weren't comfortable or they made them look different, they threw them off and went back to what was comfortable.

The problem is that outside forces are continually enlarging your comfort zone without your conscious knowledge. Look back at your life ten years ago. What's different? I'm sure there are many things now in your life that you planned for.

A bad habit never disappears miraculously — it's an undo-it-yourself project.
ꙮ ABIGAIL VAN BUREN

But how many things in your life are there because you may have been forced into a change without realizing it? Do you have new information that you read about or see when you watch television? Without knowing it, you're being pushed into a larger comfort zone.

Decide how you want to enlarge your comfort zone. See where you want to be and develop the steps necessary to be in your new "habit!" Use habits to help you realize that unless you decide to change, either you won't or forces beyond your control will!

Habit is the thing that makes us fear change, regardless
of the present condition of our lives.
ꙮ M.E. DE MONTAIGNE

Action: Write down where you'd like your sales level to be. Wherever you are right now is your comfort zone. By putting in writing where you'd really like to see your business, you subconscious mind will help you to begin to do the things necessary to expand this comfort zone.

INSANITY

*Definition of insanity, "Doing the same things over
and over again while expecting different results."*

∾ AUTHOR UNKNOWN

A young salesman loses his ring on his way to a meeting. That night, under a street lamp, he searches on his hands and knees for the ring he has lost. A friend approaches and asks what he's doing. "I'm looking for a ring I lost earlier today," he said. "Where did you lose it?" his friend asked. "About two blocks from here," said the salesman. "Why are you looking here?" quizzed his friend. The salesman replied, "Because the light is better!"

Are you selling the way you are today because the "light's better?" How many of us keep doing the same things over and over, hoping against hope, that the outcome will be different? You need to stop the way you're doing it and start to focus on the results you want, not the way you go about doing it.

The hardest thing we do is think. Experts agree that 90 percent of what we do daily is unconscious, and only about 10 percent is conscious. Because of that ratio we only do those things that are automatic. We have a very difficult time doing most of the things we do that are conscious, because we have to think, and that's hard work.

The only way we are going to change is by understanding what we know and making a conscious effort to make the change. Over 60 percent of everything we know has been presented to us at least six times. That means it may hurt to do those things that are uncomfortable, but it'll soon become a habit.

Let's conduct an experiment. Cross you arms. Okay, now uncross and recross the opposite way. Uncomfortable isn't it? That's because one day, years ago we were taught how to cross our arms. And we've done it that way ever since. If you were to cross your arms the opposite way for the next three weeks, the new way would begin to feel comfortable.

I've seen this happen in sales organizations. I'll do a training class on negotiation techniques for a group of salespeople. Let's say they believe the techniques I'm describing are so much better than the ones they've been using that they can't wait to go out and try them.

The workshop ends and they confront their first prospect since they received the new negotiation information. Which set of techniques do you think they'll use? The negotiation techniques that were just taught to them or the techniques they're most used to using? It will probably be the latter. This is one reason I suggest that after you attend a workshop, teach what you learned to somebody else because this is the best way to internalize something new. Why? Because by taking the time and effort to explain this new procedure or technique to someone totally unfamiliar with it, your subconscious mind forces this new information in deeper and helps you use it when needed.

You may not always get what you want, but you always get what you expect.

ᴓ AUTHOR UNKNOWN

Action: Begin to enlarge your comfort zone and improve a few of your current selling practices. List twelve selling habits that you'd like to change. Begin to work on one this month and continue for the next twelve months.

1. _____

2. _____

3. _____

4. _____

5. _____

6. _____

7. _____

8. _____

9. _____

10. _____

11. _____

12. _____

DEVELOPING THE LARGER COMFORT ZONE

They always say that time changes things,
but you actually have to change them yourself.
∾ ANDY WARHOL

One reason we have such a difficult time changing is because of how change occurs. We never recognize change happening, and we fear change because we don't understand it.

There's a theory that helps explain what and how change occurs. It's called the "Unconscious Incompetent." There are four steps in this process:

Unconscious Incompetent: You don't know what you don't know.

Conscious Incompetent: You know you don't know.

Conscious Competent: You know you know.

Unconscious Competent: You do it automatically.

Let's use the personal computer as an example of how this process works. Over twenty years ago you didn't know what a personal computer was because they didn't exist. You were an "unconscious incompetent." This is the way we are about things that don't yet exist.

When you saw your first personal computer you became a "conscious incompetent;" you knew you knew nothing about it. As you began using your new computer, you had to think about every move you made on the keyboard. You were a "conscious competent."

When using the computer became as natural as riding a bike and you used it without consciously thinking, you became an "unconscious competent." We begin learning by becoming aware of something we don't know. Next, we struggle through the stages of learning for the new skill to become automatic. Finally, we've internalized the information so well that the whole process becomes unconscious and habitual.

Here's an example of how this process worked for a client of mine. This client had a long-time objective to learn to speak French (he was a conscious incompetent; he knew he didn't know how to speak French). He found a French-speaking immersion class in Belgium and signed up for the ten-day program.

When he arrived in Belgium, he was told to speak only French in any communication, even though he knew very little of the language. Over the next few days, he became more frustrated with his attempts to learn French. At mealtime, he went hungry because he couldn't ask for any of the food in French. A week into the program he went back to his room frustrated. That night before falling asleep he decided he would never be able to learn French, and he was going to pack his bags the next morning and leave. This was his first night of complete rest.

After arising and packing his bags, he met a few of his colleagues on the way out. Looking conspicuous with his bags, they asked him what he was doing and where he was going. He explained everything about his frustrations and lack of ability to pick up the language . . . all in French (he became an unconscious competent)!

This is a perfect example of this process. As my client went to Belgium, he knew he didn't know the French language (conscious incompetent). Because he worked extremely hard attempting to learn (conscious competent), he hadn't realized he had actually learned the language until he was relaxed on the way out (unconscious competent).

So it is with all of us. Once we understand that there is something to learn or change (which are both the same), we then become a conscious incompetent. Beginning the learning/change process, we need to spend an enormous amount of time consciously thinking (conscious competent). This is hard work since most of our day is spent in the unconscious, reactive mode. This is where many people quit and give up.

This is the easy way out. If you were to begin a weight-lifting program tonight, tomorrow morning the muscles you weren't used to using would feel sore. There are two ways to eliminate the soreness in those muscles. One is to quit exercising the other is to keep exercising. Which one is better?

It's the same with any new process we are learning. The only thing we don't know yet is how soon we'll become an unconscious incompetent. Since we don't know when, we need to continually plow ahead focused on the result we want to achieve.

Spare me your intelligence for the next six months and do what I tell you to.
~ PAUL J. MEYER

Simply do and quit thinking about any potential problems. It's going to happen, you just don't know when. We can learn virtually everything possible, as long as we are mentally and/or physically capable.

It's imperative to be continually looking at your activity and be looking for new ways to improve. The improvements may take up to ninety days, but the improvements will come if you focus specifically on just doing the new activity. Change happens!

Two basic Rules of Life:
1) Change is inevitable
2) Everybody resists change.
ॐ RICHARD VON OECH

Action: What have you been putting off doing simply because it might be difficult to do? Is it learning a new language, breaking a habit, or maybe learning a new skill? Whatever it is you've been putting off simply because you're a conscious incompetent, make a commitment, write it down and begin to do it!

NINETY DAYS SAME AS CHANGE

We make our habits and then our habits make us.
◦ STANFORD LEE

Now that you've made the changes and you're all set to begin reaping the benefits of increased business, increased clients and increased commissions, you need to keep in mind that very little change will occur for up to three months. Why is that? Let's use an example that's easy to follow.

You decide you need to go on a diet and lose those extra twenty pounds. Today, you begin your diet and begin to take in 500 fewer calories each day. Tomorrow, you get on the scale expecting to see a drop in weight because you feel lighter since you ate less. You see that you weigh less, right? No, your body hasn't begun to accept the change since the accumulation of changes hasn't moved the needle enough yet.

This example is similar to what you'll be going through as you begin to change your behaviors and habits. You'll be doing something different, but you won't see the results that will accompany the change. Remember the old patience prayer?

Lord, please give me patience . . . and do it now!
◦ AUTHOR UNKNOWN

You need to accept the old, while you're doing the new. But don't expect miracles immediately. Once you decide to change it takes a good sixty to ninety days before you see any results. Which is why you should not think during this process, but just do. By consciously thinking about the process, you focus too much on "how" to accomplish your results and don't let this unconscious "success machine" come up with the answers for you.

The other problem that may appear to be a setback is the amount of effort you first put out and the lack of results you see. The ninety days refer to the runway time it takes to begin to see changes in the plans you've developed.

When a plane begins the take off procedure, it needs this runway time to accumulate enough speed to have the "lift" to take off. This is the time for the plane to get up enough speed to lift off. During this time, the pilot gives the plane full throttle, 100 percent power, and holds nothing back. Interestingly, a plane begins to have "lift" as soon as the pilot gives the plane full throttle. The plane just doesn't have enough power to take off, even though the plane is actually flying.

This is also similar to getting up to speed to enter the expressway. If you or the pilot gave your vehicle only half the power needed, it wouldn't be able to accomplish its purpose. The plane would crash and burn, and you wouldn't have enough speed to enter the highway.

It's the same with us. Once we develop a plan a commit to a change, we must give the plan full throttle. What's discouraging is that the plan won't actually take off for sixty to ninety days. Only then do we begin to see some kind of progress toward our objectives.

You must continue to give 100 percent of your time toward the actions necessary and be willing to not see the results for up to three months. But once the ninety days are up, you'll begin to see the whole process falling into place and slowly moving upward toward your results.

Remember that the results you are focusing on are always correct since they're the results that you want. The plan to get there may have to be altered along the way. So don't rationalize why you're not accomplishing your objectives, rather look for the changes you need to make to fix the problem and get back on track.

By focusing on the actions (once your plan is made), your subconscious mind comes up with the "how;" while your conscious mind comes up with the "what." Focusing is blocking out what's not necessary. If you focus on the "how," your subconscious mind shuts down and isn't allowed to work on the process because all the negative information is drawn in.

Let's say that last year you made $50,000. The year before you had made $25,000. You used this process and doubled your income. Now your focus is on $100,000, again doubling your income. If you focus on the "how," you begin to think of how hard you had to work to make $50,000, how hard it was to make all the sacrifices and the success machine shuts down. It becomes a self-fulfilling prophecy, and you prove to yourself that you couldn't hit $100,000 or you weren't worthy of it.

But if your focus is on the "what," regardless of what pain you went through last year, the process is actually pretty easy because your subconscious mind comes up with even more new ideas to achieve the result you're focused on! Believe in your plan and stick with it!

God's delays are not God's denials!

ᐰ ROBERT SCHULLER

Action: When do you want to see the changes you've been putting on paper throughout this book? Write down ninety days from today as your change objective.

90-Day Objective Date: _____

TENTH MULTIPLE

If you continue as you have in the past, where will you be five years from now?
Ꮑ AUTHOR UNKNOWN

There's a concept used in financial planning called "The Tenth Multiple." It's used to help investors weather the slow process of becoming financially independent and/or hitting specific financial objectives. The same concept can be used as you're working toward hitting your specific sales objective.

The tenth multiple shows that once you develop your sales plan, simply work the plan. By focusing on making the plan work, your efforts begin to double your results over time. By continually doubling, you can plan out how long it will take to reach your objective.

As you can see in the illustration that follows, when you double $1,000 ten times you'll have over $1 million.

Start with $1,000. Double the value ten times:
1) $2000
2) $4000
3) $8000
4) $16,000
5) $32,000 - Half Way
6) $64,000
7) $128,000
8) $256,000
9) $512,000
10) $1,024,000

(SUCCESS MOTIVATION INSTITUTE, WACO, TX)

Here's what makes the tenth multiple so interesting. How much money do you have at the halfway point? Only $32,000! You've spent half the time and are only 3.2 percent of the way there. Let's say you tell a friend of yours that in ten years you'll have $1 million. You haven't seen this friend in five years, and when you get together, your friend asks how you're doing toward your $1 million. You tell your friend, "Great, I have $32,000!" What's your friend going to do? Probably laugh. The average person has absolutely no comprehension on how this process works.

Let's relate this to your sales situation. You begin making ten additional phone calls every day. You may get real lucky and have most of the ten calls become appointments, but in most cases, those ten calls are probably going to be learning experiences at first.

What begins to happen is that your activity and behavior have changed, but your attitude, emotions and skill level are still at the old behavior level and have yet to catch up. What you're doing is enlarging that comfort zone.

The man who removes a mountain begins by carrying away small stones.
    ∾ CHINESE PROVERB

Action: Based on the tenth multiple theory, develop a plan for yourself. It may be financially based, career oriented or some other plan. Develop a plan using the ten steps. Write down where you'll be at each step until you hit number ten, which is your final objective.

Would you accomplish every one of the items below if you knew that when you completed the last one you'd have the results and the success you wanted? If you said "yes" then develop your plan, work on it and enjoy your success!

1. _____

_____

2. _____

_____

3. _____

_____

4. _____

_____

5. _____

_____

6. _____

_____

7. _____

_____

8. _____

_____

9. _____

_____

10. _____

_____

NEXT

Wisdom oft times consists of knowing what to do next.
꙰ HERBERT HOOVER

The most important word in being successful is "next." When you don't know what comes next, you tend to stand still, do nothing and procrastinate.

Many people are continually being directed and programmed by a series of crisis situations, rather than a planned program of actions. Procrastination develops and continues when an individual has no idea of what to do step-by-step. By knowing what comes next, you're able to develop a plan of action.

A number of years ago, I decided to put a remote keypad outside my garage door. I purchased the unit, and it sat on my desk for about three months. Why? I didn't know how to install the unit. I didn't know what came "next." In a fit of passion one Sunday after football season was over, I opened the box and much to my surprise, inside was a set of instructions. Aside from having to splice two wires together, the procedure was relatively simple. It took all of thirty minutes for the project, and I walked around the house beating my chest like Tarzan, looking for additional projects to do.

Why did I feel that way? Having a set of instructions is much the same as having a game plan to achieve results. If I could write down a list of step-by-step instructions of exactly what you had to do to achieve your results (similar to what you just accomplished in the previous action step), and I told you to just follow each step and not go on to the next one until the one before was completed, would you be excited? Of course you would. This will never happen, but you can do it for yourself. One of the biggest reasons why you haven't accomplished whatever it is you want to accomplish is simply because you haven't decided what comes next.

As you develop your sales objectives, write out a step-by-step plan to achieve whatever objectives you're going after. Will the step-by-step formula guarantee success? Of course not! But it will guarantee that you will begin to make the movements toward success. If you don't quit, you'll simply keep revising the plan until you've accomplished your results.

A measure of success is not a question of judging yourself compared to someone else, but a question of judging yourself against your own potential.

∾ GEORGE ROMNEY

Action: What comes next? Continue to develop your step-by-step plan to achieve your sales success. Write down your sales objective for this year (you developed this number earlier in Part Four). Next, write out a few action steps with deadlines to move you toward achieving your objective.

Objective:_____

Action Steps	Deadline
1. _____	_____
2. _____	_____
3. _____	_____
4. _____	_____
5. _____	_____
6. _____	_____
7. _____	_____
8. _____	_____
9. _____	_____
10. _____	_____

ATTITUDES/ACTIVITIES/SKILLS

The best investment one can make in life is to invest in oneself. If a man empties his purse into his head, no one can take it away from him.

∾ BENJAMIN FRANKLIN

How do you develop these strong objectives, the charisma and leadership skills necessary to achieve fantastic results? Use the "Salt Theory."

You've heard the expression, "You can lead a horse to water, but you can't make him drink." In actuality, you can add one more part to that phrase " . . . unless you can make the horse awfully damn thirsty!"

Most salespeople have no idea how to develop strong motivation. Everyone wants something or some things. It's your job to find out exactly what your motivators are, which may be deeply hidden.

The job of a salesperson is to uncover the prospect's wants or "gap." Salespeople accomplish this by asking questions. In this way, the salesperson can help paint a picture of what the prospect wants. That's what people buy—what they see and believe.

Salespeople must understand how to do this also to and for themselves. You need to uncover your needs and wants to realize your full potential.

Let's review "Skills/Activities/Attitudes from Part One. When you have a sales problem—let's say an inability to negotiate the sale—many salespeople will attempt to work on negotiation skills. Once the salesperson thinks it's fixed, then the salesperson works on increasing their sales activity so they can handle more negotiations. Finally, the salesperson works on developing the right attitudes for effective negotiations.

In reality, this process works in reverse. Assuming a negotiation problem, check your attitude first. Almost every problem associated with selling has to do with habits of thinking, or attitudes. Only after you understand how you are thinking should you move on to the next step—activity.

Generally, salespeople know more than they apply when it comes to sales skills. It's really the attitude that they have about the skill or the product that keeps them from selling correctly. But again, once that attitude is adjusted (and this is a daily process for most salespeople) then it's just a matter of increasing your activity for the skill to be internalized.

How do you learn to set appointments, make presentations or negotiate a sale? You learn by doing these activities as often as possible and as close together as possible. Ask for the order a thousand times and you'll learn how to negotiate. You don't learn how to negotiate from waiting to get the right prospect, at the right time, with enough money and who wants to buy your product/service today.

Only those who risk going too far can possibly find how far they can go.

∿ AUTHOR UNKNOWN

Action: How's your attitude? Write down whatever areas of sales you'd like to improve or are possibly having problems with. Next, write down what you feel you should be doing to correct and/or improve your sales situation. Ask yourself why you aren't doing this. Once you realize there's nothing to hold you back ... just do it!

Sales Areas	Activity Level
1. _____	_____
2. _____	_____
3. _____	_____
4. _____	_____
5. _____	_____

SUCCESS DEGREES

Success is not how far you have to travel,
but the distance you've traveled from the start.

∾ AUTHOR UNKNOWN

Are you successful right now? Absolutely! You've achieved a certain degree of success by what you've accomplished up to this point. But you may believe you are not successful simply because you haven't had the success you want to achieve—because you may not have earned the right to reach that level yet.

You haven't earned the right possibly because you haven't yet had enough setbacks. Until you've understood and experienced the opposite of success (setbacks), it's very difficult to understand the meaning of success. The opposite of success is not failure. Failure is simply giving up. Your ability to be successful is directly related to your ability to overcome setbacks. If you failed in sales, it's simply because you quit!

A preacher once said, "Opposites are proof of each other."

You can't have life without death. You can't have love without hate. And you can't have success without setbacks. To truly understand what it takes to become successful, you have to have a taste of true setbacks first.

What most people think is failure is simply not trying or maybe having a slight setback. Not making a sale after seeing twenty prospects does not mean you can't be a salesperson. It simply means you haven't learned enough yet from your setbacks to enjoy the fruits of true failure or success.

During the late 1980s, I was successful since I had been the top salesperson most of that decade. I wasn't number one, however, because I was the best. I was on top because no one else was making the effort to truly compete with me.

During this time, I began accumulating a tremendous amount of debt. This was a major concern not only because of the debt, but because the business I was in promoted success. Here I was with the outer trappings of success, but behind the scenes I was struggling to make ends meet. I hadn't yet earned the right to be truly successful because I hadn't truly had the taste of failure.

I was told I should file for bankruptcy. I considered it, but I realized that by filing bankruptcy I was admitting defeat and failure. I accumulated the debt. I was going to pay off the debt. The only way out was to admit where I was and to look at my entire life and career totally differently. If I were to be successful it would only happen after I decided to change.

This is probably what an alcoholic goes through. I've never even been a heavy drinker, but I've had enough reformed alcoholics as clients to know that before you can become a reformed alcoholic, you must first admit to being an alcoholic.

It's similar to success. Before you can become successful, you first need to admit that where you are and what you are doing is not where you want to be. Once that decision is made (and it's a decision that may be easy on the surface but difficult to implement), you can begin to outline your change.

We're all familiar with the biblical story of Moses parting the Red Sea. Something very similar happens once you've made the critical decision to change. Your mind becomes extremely clear as to what new decisions need to be made. New ideas begin to come to you, and the new ideas begin to make sense. The way is now clear to begin day one of your new life.

Part of my problem was that I was focusing on the debt and not the way out of the debt. By deciding to change, my focus began to change.

I was receiving "dunning" calls daily. When you are receiving calls from creditors asking you to pay your bills and you can't pay them, it's very difficult to go out and sell!

Since the decision to change had been made, ideas began to surface. I first decided to collect the debt that was owed to me. I had been extending credit to clients as quickly as creditors were extending it to me. My faith in my clients exceeded my faith in myself to pay back the debt.

I suggested to my secretary that she begin to "nice" our clients to death! She began a volley of phone calls to these clients, and as nice as she could be, asked when they could pay all or part of their debt. She would also ask when they thought they would be sending a check. She then went on to ask permission to call back after the check should have arrived, if it hadn't.

We all know the "squeaky wheel" gets the grease. That's exactly what began to happen. My clients began to send checks because they knew that my secretary was going to keep calling and not let up until they did. She was like a doberman pinscher in her relentlessness in calling and being nice.

Next, I had to handle all of the lines of credit due. The volume of debt I was under felt stifling. I needed desperately to get the debt under control. Step one was to call every creditor and let them know my situation. I had my secretary make these calls and let them know that she was going to call twice a month. The first call was to let the creditor know exactly how much I was going to pay that month (some payments were as low as $5). The second call was made after she had come back from the post office to let the creditor know the check had just been mailed. Every call coming from these creditors stopped!

Imagine the relief of knowing that no creditor was calling looking for a payment. Now I could go out and sell to make the money to pay these creditors. All creditors want two things: to get paid and for you to stay in touch with them should there be a problem. I decided to stay in touch by calling twice a month and paying each of them at least a small sum monthly.

But to keep the cards active, you need to make at least the minimum payment monthly. I wasn't able to do this, and since most of the open lines of credit were credit cards, and these creditors were not getting paid as much as they wanted each month, all were cancelled except two. I had kept up payments on these two cards, so at least I had two walking-around cards. (In retrospect, they actually did me a favor by canceling all of the other lines of credit.)

Now that payments were being made and the process was under control, I wanted to find a way to reduce the amount of interest I was paying. Even though I was making some kind of monthly payment to every creditor, the payments were so small that I was actually increasing my debt because of the interest being tacked on monthly. The interest rates were all in the neighborhood of 18%–24%.

Since I was thinking more clearly, my next idea was to consolidate these outstanding bills. Since my credit wasn't very good at the time and I still wasn't making the kind of money I needed to yet, I looked at a few unconventional, yet legal sources of consolidation. I was able to find one source that would pay every line of credit off at an interest rate that wouldn't burden me monthly. Not only did I have the debt under control now, but I also had only one creditor who was willing to let me spread the payments out over a few years to be able to handle the monthly payment.

I originally decided on this change with the objective of being 100 percent clear of all debt within five years. Though the plan was working out and the income was rising, I hadn't taken into account that along the way, I still needed to spend money to live. My program took longer than expected.

My income began to rise because not only was I able to make more sales, since I didn't have the pressure of debt, but the types of sales I was making began to change. At this time, I was selling primarily to individuals with a few companies using my services for workshops. I preferred the workshops since I was paid more and I could use my talents more effectively.

The debt was finally paid off 8½ years after the objective was set, 3½ years longer than originally planned. But it happened, and the ability to become more successful increased a hundredfold, as a result of hitting (what I thought) was bottom. Without that experience, I would never have been able to experience the success I achieved to that point. To become truly successful, you need to experience the setbacks.

*All life demands struggle. Those who have everything given to them become
lazy, selfish, and insensitive to the real values of life. The very striving
and hard work that we so constantly try to avoid is the major building
block in the person we are today.*

*Too often we try to get something for nothing. We want to go through
life without paying the price. How many people never really learn their jobs,
never ask questions, and don't know their line of work? We have become
a people who take the easy way out. We don't demand anything of ourselves.
We don't struggle to draw out more of the latent potential that God
placed in the innermost recesses of our mind.*

*Without struggle there is no progress, no greatness, no making of things
to happen. To grasp this principle is to grasp life. Struggle is a law so basic to
building a better person, so fundamental to building a better world, that is
amazing how few people know its value. Before the reward there must be labor.
You plant before you harvest. You sow in tears before you reap in joy.*

∾ "STEPS ON THE STAIRWAY" BY RALPH RANSOM

Action: What setbacks have occurred in your life? Write them down. Realizing that not everything has happened correctly in your life may aid in your movement toward the success you'd like to attain.

1. _____

_____

2. _____

_____

3. _____

_____

4. _____

_____

5. _____

_____

PASSION

> *We may affirm absolutely that nothing great in the world*
> *has ever been accomplished without passion.*
>
> ～ GEORG HEGEL

What kept me working toward my objective? As a matter of fact, what keeps most individuals on track to achieve without quitting? In a word, passion. Enjoy what you do so much that you would never consider quitting.

We've all heard the term "burnout," and the biggest reason it happens is because of a lack of focus on specific objectives. When you enjoy and love what you're doing, you generally don't burn out. You don't burn out because your focus is always on doing something you enjoy doing.

If you don't enjoy what you're doing, go out and find something to do that fires your passion. You're doing your employer and yourself a disservice by staying in your position.

The test to determine whether you have the passion for what it is you're doing is to be willing to do your job for no pay if you were financially well off. I'll ask individuals what they'd do if they won a lottery. Almost everyone says, "Quit my job." I tell them if that's what they'd do, then quit now and find something that gets you excited.

Should you ever win a lottery, you're still going to have to do something to fill your time. Figure out what that is and find a way to do it! That "something" is the activity that gets you excited; that fuels your passion. Passion is wanting something so badly that nothing will stop you from getting it.

Have you ever wanted to go out on a date with someone so badly that you did whatever it took to get that individual to go out with you? Or was there ever something in your life that you wanted so badly that you moved heaven and earth just to make it happen? That's passion!

> *There is some one thing that you can do better than anyone else*
> *in the world could do it. Search until you find out what this particular*
> *line of endeavor is, make it the object of your definite chief aim and then*
> *organize all of your forces and attack it with the belief that you are going*
> *to win. In your search for the work for which you are best fitted, it will*

be well if you bear in mind the fact that you will most likely attain the greatest success by finding out what work you like best, for it is a well-known fact that a man generally best succeeds in the particular line of endeavor into which he can throw his whole heart and soul.

～ NAPOLEAN HILL FROM "LAWS OF SUCCESS"

Action: What's your real passion? What is it that gets your motor running? Write it down, and figure out what it will take to do it or more of it.

My Passion: _____

_____

How will I do more to get it? _____

_____

RISKING

If you cannot risk, you cannot grow, you cannot become your best. If you cannot become your best, you cannot be happy. If you cannot be happy, what else matters?

∽ AUTHOR UNKNOWN

All progress and growth involves risk. The questions you need to ask yourself are: "What's the worst than can happen?" and "What's the worst that can happen to me?" You must know your upside potential based on your downside risk. Your upside potential has an objective you want to achieve. If you're willing to risk whatever that downside risk is, then you're going to go for what you want to have.

But it hurts to risk, because when you risk, you're going against status quo. You're going against what you are used to doing. You're going against change. You're expanding your "comfort zone." You must deal now with the obstacles that stand between you and what you want to have. Most of those obstacles are between your ears. These are the challenges that are going to cause you to stretch.

A physical muscle once stretched never goes back to where it was before. You can become flabby after not using that muscle, but the muscle once stretched stays at its new form. A mental and emotional muscle once stretched never goes back to where it was before, either.

Risk involves pain or hurt. You can't lift weights without having weights. You have to push against something. As mentioned before, have you ever awakened in the morning after a new exercise and felt sore? At that point, you have two choices. You can quit exercising and the pain goes away. Or you can keep exercising, and the pain goes away. The end results are similar, but one is going to make you feel a lot better.

You have to stay with it to get the full exhilaration. The more you love security, the more likely you will avoid risk and you also avoid opportunity. Because risk is the price you pay for opportunity. You can't hate risk and hope for freedom. Risk is an essential part of progress.

What is success? How does success tie into risk? Again, success is a series of setbacks leading to positive results. There cannot be success without setbacks. As we've discussed before, opposites are proof of each other.

How you think when you lose determines how long it will be until you win.
∾ DAVID SCHULTZ FROM "THE MAGIC OF THINKING BIG"

To be successful you must have setbacks. You must expect the best but plan for the worst. Any growth involves taking risks. If you never make a mistake, never experience a setback or never encounter an obstacle, you are not growing, not improving and not experiencing.

The key is to know which risk to take and which risks to avoid. This is to understand how to assess the possible consequences. Match them with your ability, then act with confidence.

The bumblebee cannot fly because of the shape and weight of its
body in relation to the total wing area. But the bumblebee doesn't
know this so it goes ahead and flies anyway.
∾ AUTHOR UNKNOWN

Action: What risks are you taking now? A risk can be as simple as doing something you've never done before. All risks hurt because we've never been there before and they're outside of our "comfort zone." Write out five things that you'd like to do that you've always talked about doing someday.

1. _____

_____

2. _____

_____

3. _____

_____

4. _____

_____

5. _____

_____

COMMITMENT

You don't last long if you're not willing to make a commitment.
    ∾ JACK PALANCE

The following story will help you understand why you shouldn't turn back once you make a commitment to your results.

The chicken and the pig were walking down the street when they saw a diner with a sign that read, "Ham and Eggs, 99 cents." The chicken said that the reason ham and eggs were so popular was because of the chicken. The chicken lays the eggs and people enjoy eggs.

The pig replied, "You may have a point, but remember, a chicken's only involved, a pig's committed!"

Self-motivated people make commitments, ordinary people make promises.
    ∾ AUTHOR UNKNOWN

Commit to what? Commit to action, commit to work, commit to win, commit to your clients, but even more importantly, commit to you. The one person that you break commitments to more than anyone else is yourself. When you commit to yourself and stick to your commitment, then you are going to commit to others, and you are going to make it happen.

There's tremendous power in commitment. It forces you to think and to come up with ways to make your objective achievable. Self-motivated and objective-directed actions reinforce your commitment. Commitment is a habit. It's a strand of string that would break if pulled. But instead, every day you add one more strand and another and another, until one day you pull on the string and it's become a rope and it can't be broken.

Your "rope" is what happens when you have a habit of commitment.

*The quality of a person's life is in direct proportion to their commitment
to excellence, regardless of their chosen field of endeavor.*

∾ VINCE LOMBARDI

Action: Go ahead, make a commitment!

THE "SLIGHT EDGE"

*Fight one more round. When your feet are so tired that you have to shuffle
back to the corner of the ring, fight one more round. When your
arms are so tired that you can hardly lift your hands to come on guard,
fight one more round. When your nose is bleeding and your eyes
are black and you are so tired that you wish your opponent would crack
you one on the jaw and put you to sleep, fight one more round; remembering
that the man who always fights one more round is never whipped.*

∾ JAMES J. CORBETT

The "slight edge" is about attitudes. Attitudes are habits of thought. It's the way you think about what you do. It's the way you think that lets your prospect pull their "lid" down.

Attitudes are based on how you think of yourself and how you perceive your environment. Reality is simply your perception. You can choose to believe anything you want to believe.

Your "slight edge" is the way you believe and think. Winners believe, no matter what happens and no matter how long, they will persevere. Winning is a habit, just like losing is a habit. Their "slight edge" gives them just that "little bit more" than most other individuals have. The "slight edge" isn't much in attitude or thinking, but it's just enough to make the difference between a successful salesperson and a mediocre salesperson.

*. . . it's general knowledge that 20 percent of all the salespeople
make 80 percent of all the sales. Immediately these disproportionate
figures indicate that a salesperson in the top 20 percent sells at
a rate of 16 times higher than those in the lower 20 percent. And we
marvel at the ant who can pull eight times his own weight.*

∾ ROBERT L. SHOOK FROM "WE ALL SELL . . . BUT SOME SELL BETTER. WHY?"

This difference between success and failure is usually only slight. All you've read about in this book is designed to help develop your "slight edge," in order to more effectively achieve your results. As mentioned, when you're one of a hundred salespeople competing for the top prize, you're actually only competing with two or three others. Most salespeople in that large a group don't believe they'll win, so they don't even try. Here are two examples:

    a) The difference in salaries between baseball players can be great based on the number of their hits. Top salaries are given to players who hit over .300 compared to players hitting around .200 . . . one more hit at bat out of every ten.

    b) Golfers who win the most tournaments are only a few strokes under most other players, but the difference in their incomes is enormous; just because of the difference of a few strokes.

Developing this slight edge is imperative in the way you handle yourself and your activity. Sometimes, success is only one more phone call each day, one more sales call each week or one more referral from each person you talk to. We're not talking about results, we're talking about the activity (which you have total control over) to get those results.

So what are the attitudes and the "slight edge" of a winner? What attitudes do winners have that cause them to be winners? Here are five:

    1) Winners are prepared. They are prepared ahead of time.

    2) Winners have a positive expectancy to win. They believe in advance that they are going to make it happen.

    3) Winners are specific and they are positive about their winning.

    4) Winners accept personal responsibility for their actions . . . "It's my fault and nobody else's." They pay the price willingly because they know it's a bargain.

    5) Winners achieve their objectives.

By developing the ability to commit, you begin to develop your "slight edge." Your true "slight edge" is your ability to help your prospects "pull down their garbage can lid" so that you can begin to "see the whites of their eyes!" This is where the trust between you and your prospect begins. This is the "slight edge" that separates you from the majority of salespeople on the street.

As you've read *Sell When You See the Whites of Their Eyes!* you began to understand your (1) Attitudes and how to adjust them to increase your sales. You also began to (2) Track your results so that you would be able to focus your efforts on achieving your objectives.

After you developed your selling process into (3) Nine Steps, you saw how important it was to follow each step and get permission to continue from your prospect. You also incorporated (4) Change into your sales arsenal by developing the attitudes and behaviors to work for you rather than against you.

And, finally, by putting your ACTION steps on paper and developing plans to achieve your objectives from the four sections of this book, you have successfully understood how to help your prospect pull down their imaginary "garbage can lids," and you now are selling by "seeing the whites of their eyes!"

This is the "slight edge." This is the magic of selling.

As I paused to think of something that sets us all apart
It seemed to me that objectives in life must be the place to start.
Imagine playing football on an unmarked field of green
Not a goal line to be sought, not a goal post to be seen.
It would be an aimless battle, were there nothing to be gained
Without a thing to strive for, not a score to be attained.
We must have a purpose in our lives, for the flame that warms the soul
Is an everlasting vision, all of us must have a goal.

∾ AUTHOR UNKNOWN

Set the objective, have the courage and make it happen!

Action No. 1: What's your slight edge? What's that one thing you do that makes you different from every other salesperson who calls on your prospect or client? Write down your slight edge, and write down how you're going to act upon it.

Slight Edge:

Action Plan:

Action No. 2: If you've followed through on all of the action steps throughout this book, you have, not only a tremendous amount of information written both in this book, but also on your own sheets of paper. Now is the time to go through all that you have written and begin to put your action steps for improvement in action. Pick a daily time to review and to work on your action steps.

My daily planning time: _____

18 KEYS TO REMEMBER DURING THE CRITICAL SALES CONFRONTATION:

1) **Seven Objections.** When your prospect objects, you haven't given sufficient reason to buy. All your prospect is doing is asking for these reasons. So let your prospect have them and keep negotiating. Your prospect won't take offense when you ask for the order, but they will if it's wanted and you quit too early. What if your prospect objects seven times? Either you're talking to the wrong person (anyone can say no), or your prospect really means it!

2) **Keep Selling.** No matter what happens, keep selling. Be it interruptions, an objection or inattentiveness . . . keep selling!

3) **Ask Questions.** You'll never know what your prospect wants unless you ask questions. Make your prospect tell you what their needs and desires are. By doing so, your prospect will buy and you won't have to sell.

4) **Keep Selling.** Are you a professional visitor or a professional salesperson? You have a saleable product/service that is either going to make your prospect happy, rich, enlarge their ego or all three. You prospect wants it . . . keep selling!

5) **Why?** When all else fails or your prospect states an objection, make them tell you why. Just ask!

6) **Keep Selling.** Remember the food that goes on your table is in direct proportion to what you take with you right now.

7) **In Addition To That?** After your prospect states the objection, ask: "In addition to that, is there any other reason why you wouldn't buy?" If your prospect says no, answer the objection and negotiate. Your prospect told you to. If they say yes, find out the other objections, answer them and negotiate.

8) **Keep Selling.** Don't let your ego get in the way. When your prospect objects, it's not an objection to you, it's an objection to your product, service or idea. Keep selling and find the reason.

9) **Assumptive Negotiation.** How do you ask for the order? Assume your prospect will buy. Ask your either-or question: "Would you like it in red or blue?" "Is one gross enough or would you like two?" "Would you like it delivered Monday or Tuesday?" Remember, whenever your prospect asks a question, answer with a question. The person asking the question always is in control. "Can I have it in red?" "Do you want it in red?

10) **Keep Selling.** Your prospect granted you this interview because they were interested in your product, service or idea. In the back of their mind,

there was that chance that your prospect might need what you have. Don't stop . . . they need it, they just don't know it yet.

11) **Listen.** After you ask a question . . . LISTEN! Just sit there with your note pad and pen. Take notes and ask questions when your prospect stops talking, but listen because somewhere in that answer or objection is the reason they want to buy. Your prospect won't tell you, they're asking you to find the reason because they may not know themselves. They want your help.

12) **Keep Selling.** Keep throwing those benefits at them. Tell them what it's going to do for them or their family or their business. Why should your prospect buy?

13) **Answer A Question With A Question.** Drop statements from your vocabulary. Anytime you make a statement, you're running the risk of offending your prospect. If you have no choice but to make a statement, end it by asking, "Right?" Let them do the talking . . . they're selling themselves. Don't make your prospect feel that they've bought, because they won't.

14) **Keep Selling.** Your prospect will sell you whenever they can. They're good at it. It's your job to be empathetic rather than sympathetic. Understand how your prospect feels, but stay back; don't get involved with their feelings; otherwise, you're dead. Rather, remain aloof, understand the problem and help solve it with your product or service.

15) **Ask For Payment.** Two reasons: One, your probability of keeping the order and not having it cancelled is improved if the money is in your pocket ahead if time. Your prospect is asked this question daily and so are you every time you make a purchase at any retail store. Two, you've helped your prospect establish their credit rating. Eventually, getting the money is the actual completion of the order. Why not get paid now during a positive meeting rather than a negative one, especially should they get behind on their payments?

16) **Keep Selling.** You have everything to offer. Take your time, present your ideas logically and answer objections, but most of all, keep selling!

17) **Be Imaginative.** Be different, make your prospect a part of your presentation, make them do some work, let them calculate. Keep thinking of a way to get your points across in the most unique way you can.

18) **Keep Selling.** Always sell and negotiate on something. Sell your product or service. If you can't do that now, sell your next meeting, sell the next time you'll call, sell the next follow-up or possibly sell them on getting referrals. But always remember: Keep Selling!

Seven Objections

Keep Selling!

Ask Questions

Keep Selling!

Why?

Keep Selling!

In Addition To That?

Keep Selling!

Assumptive Negotiation

Keep Selling!

Listen

Keep Selling!

Answer A Question With A Question

Keep Selling!

Ask For Payment

Keep Selling!

Be Imaginative

KEEP SELLING!

Action: Congratulations on taking the time and effort to begin your journey of success and improvement. One of the most successful methods of guaranteeing your success is to commit your change to others.

To help you make that commitment, write a letter telling of your success and/or changes that you're going to make a commitment to. The act of writing the letter will speed you toward additional success!

Send your letter to:

Steve A Klein

Professional Development Center

Box 852076

Richardson, TX 75085-2076

   -Or-

E-mail: saklein@earthlink.net

---

*Until you are committed, there is hesitancy, the chance to
draw back, always ineffectiveness.*

*Concerning all acts of initiative and creation, there is one
elementary truth, the ignorance of which kills countless ideas and
splendid plans. The truth is this: that the moment you definitely
commit yourself, then Providence moves too.*

*All sorts of things occur to help you, things that would never
have otherwise occurred. A whole stream of events issues from your decision.
They raise in your favor all manner of unforeseen incidents and
meetings and material assistance, which no man could have
dreamed would come your way.*

Whatever you can do, or dream you can do, then begin it.

Boldness has genius, power and magic in it. Begin it now, to be bold!

              ❧ JOHANN WOLFGANG VON GOETHE 1796

"IT'S IN YOUR HANDS" FABLE

Once upon a time there was a wise man who lived near a village, far, far away, on top of the highest mountain. He was reported to be the wisest man from far and wide. People went to him for counsel, and he was wise in his advice.

But there was also a young man who had heard about this wise man and felt he could fool him by trapping the wise man into giving incorrect information. His plan was to capture a bird and take it to the old wise man. He would hold the bird behind his back and ask, "Old man, what do I have in my hands?" The young man hoped the wise man would say, "Since I see feathers behind your back, you must have a bird." This young man would then ask, "But is this bird dead or alive?" If the wise man said the bird was "dead," the young man would let the bird fly away. But if the wise man said the bird was "alive," the young man would crush the bird in his hands and produce a dead bird!

This young man set off to find a bird and make the trek to see this wise man. After a long journey searching to find the wise man, the young man finally stood in front of him and asked, "Wise man, what do I have in my hands?" The old man replied, "A bird." Excited that he was about to trap and fool the old man, the young man then asked, "But is this bird dead or alive?" The wise man looked at the boy, paused a moment, and then said, "Son, you hold the answer in your own hands!"

You didn't just stumble onto the great treasures of life, or find them by accident. You found them because you were searching for them. The easy shortcuts to success lead nowhere.

What looks obvious must be found. What looks easy must be worked for.
    RALPH RANSOM FROM "STEPS ON THE STAIRWAY"

Appendix

Sell When You See the Whites of Their Eyes!

1) CHART OF ACCOUNTS

		Monthly Minimum	Monthly Maximum
Fixed	Rent or Mortgage	_____	_____
Expenses	Utilities	_____	_____
	Disability Insurance	_____	_____
	Fire/General Insurance	_____	_____
	Income/State Tax	_____	_____
	Property Taxes	_____	_____
	Social Security	_____	_____
	Telephone	_____	_____
	Other	_____	_____
Living	Food	_____	_____
Expenses	Clothing/Footwear	_____	_____
	Laundry/Tailor	_____	_____
	Nonbusiness Meals	_____	_____
	Auto - Nonbusiness	_____	_____
	Doctor/Dentist	_____	_____
	Prescriptions	_____	_____
	Other	_____	_____
Savings	Life Insurance	_____	_____
	Savings Account	_____	_____
	Debt Reduction	_____	_____
	Investments	_____	_____
	Other	_____	_____
Misc.	Tithe/Charities	_____	_____
	Vacation/Entertainment	_____	_____
	Club/Dues	_____	_____
	Gifts/Services	_____	_____
	Other	_____	_____

Total Income Required: _____ _____

X12   X12

Total Income Yearly: _____ _____

Sell When You See the Whites of Their Eyes!

2) BUSINESS ACCOUNTS

	Monthly Minimum	**Monthly Maximum**
Accounting	_____	_____
Advertising/Contests/Promotion	_____	_____
Business Note Payments	_____	_____
Entertainment	_____	_____
Interest/Bank Charges	_____	_____
Office Rental/Meeting Rooms	_____	_____
Personal Development	_____	_____
Postage	_____	_____
Printing/Stationery	_____	_____
Secretarial/Answering Service	_____	_____
Taxes/Licenses	_____	_____
Telephone	_____	_____
Travel/Transportation	_____	_____
Miscellaneous	_____	_____
Other	_____	_____

Total Income Required: _____ _____

X12 X12

Total Business Income: _____ _____

\+ \+

Total Personal Income: _____ _____
(From the last section)

= =

Total Income Objective: _____ _____

Sell When You See the Whites of Their Eyes!

3) WEEKLY PLANNING GUIDE

	Monday	Tuesday	Wednesday	Thursday	Friday	Saturday
7:00						
7:30						
8:00						
8:30						
9:00						
9:30						
10:00						
10:30						
11:00						
11:30						
12:00						
12:30						
1:00						
1:30						
2:00						
2:30						
3:00						
3:30						
4:00						
4:30						
5:00						
5:30						
6:00						

Sell When You See the Whites of Their Eyes!

4) DAILY SALES ACTIVITIES

Activity	(Objective) #Yearly	#Monthly	#Weekly	#Daily	Success Target
1.					
2.					
3.					
4.					
5.					
6.					
7.					
8.					
9.					
10.					

Sell When You See the Whites of Their Eyes!

5) CORRECT, CONSISTENT DAILY ACTIVITY—SCOREKEEPING

Week: Activity:	(1) Contacts	(2) Appts	(3) Pres	(4) Negotiations	(5) Sales	(6) Leads	(7) $s	(8) #s
Points:								
ST:								
Objective:								
Monday:								
Tuesday:								
Wednesday:								
Thursday:								
Friday:								
Saturday:								
Total:								
Total Points:								

6) CCDA RATIOS

	This Week	Last Week	This Month	Last Month
1) Total Commission Earned:				
2) Negotiating Average (Column 5/4):				
3) Earning per Presentation:				
4) Contacts to Appointments (2/1):				
5) Appointment to Sales (Column 5/2):				
6) Cancellation Ratio (Column 2/3):				
7) Sales to Presentations (Column 5/3):				
8) Contacts to Sales (Column 5/1):				
9) $ Value of Each Contact (Commissions/1):				

7) SUCCESS CHECKLIST

I) Objectives

	Yes	No
1) Weekly income objective of $ _____	_____	_____
2) Weekly sales objective of $ _____	_____	_____

II) Prospects

1) _____ new prospects daily _____ _____
2) _____ referrals after each sale _____ _____
3) Adequate information on each referral _____ _____
4) Used three prospecting methods daily _____ _____
5) Used the prospect system daily _____ _____

III) Contacts

1) Called at same place and time daily _____ _____
2) Prepared _____ prospect cards before phone time _____ _____
3) Used a planned telephone approach _____ _____
4) Used the CCDA tracking report _____ _____
5) Contacted _____ new prospects daily _____ _____
6) Made at least _____ new appointments daily _____ _____

IV) Presentations

1) Planned each presentation _____ _____
2) Completed each presentation in allotted time _____ _____
3) Reassured with confidence _____ _____
4) Met negotiation objective of _____% _____ _____
5) Genuinely interested in client's needs _____ _____
6) Good listener _____ _____

V) Self-Management

1) Used weekly plan sheet daily _____ _____
2) Scheduled appointments geographically _____ _____
3) Know how much an hour is worth _____ _____
4) Used to-do list daily _____ _____

VI) Attitude

1) Used verbal statements and visualization daily _____ _____
2) Worked on improving one specific selling skill _____ _____
3) Positive mental attitude toward business _____ _____
4) Have I "seen the whites of their eyes?" _____ _____

VII) Product Knowledge

1) Adequate, detailed product knowledge _____ _____
2) Spend 15 minutes/day learning _____ _____

Sell When You See the Whites of Their Eyes!

8) MRO CHART

MRO (Minimum/Realistic/Optimistic)

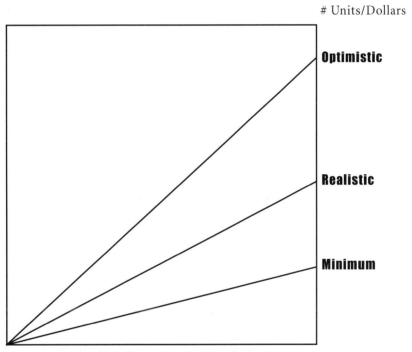

Sell When You See the Whites of Their Eyes!

ORDER FORM

To order additional copies of *Sell When You See the Whites of Their Eyes!*:

Price: $29.95 plus $3.00 shipping fee. Texas residents add 8.25% sales tax.

Name: _____

Address: _____

_____

City: _____ State: _____ Zip: _____

Daytime Phone: (____) _____ No. of Copies: _____

E-mail: _____

☐ Check or Money Order: Amount Enclosed: $ _____

☐ VISA   ☐ Mastercard   ☐ AMEX   _____

Expiration Date: _____ Signature _____

Mail To: Professional Development Center
             Box 852076
             Richardson, TX 75085-2076

Phone: (972) 644-1048
Fax: (972) 234-8764

Sell When You See the Whites of Their Eyes!

Steve A Klein

Biography

Steve A Klein of the Professional Development Center in Richardson, Texas, has generated a diverse range of professional training and consultation programs and has a strong background in personal development training.

He graduated from Northern Illinois University with a bachelor of arts in the fields of speech communication and broadcast journalism. He worked for ten years in radio and television, both on-air and behind the camera. He took an indirect step into sales and soon realized that the selling profession was his passion. Klein began his own company in 1980 and worked with one organization achieving top sales status seven years in a row.

Klein's company, the Professional Development Center, has performed extensive training for such companies as Southwest Airlines, the United States Marine Corps, Chrysler, Ericsson, Nissan, Ford and The Dallas Morning News. His training focuses on such key issues as relationship leadership, team building, sales management, sales negotiation, tracking and prospecting, customer service, self-management, communication skills, and cultural and behavior change. He has been a part of numerous satellite television broadcasts and expanded his operations through audio and videotapes, allowing small and medium-sized companies, as well as Fortune 500 and Fortune 1000 companies, to implement his techniques.

A volunteer for Adopt-a-School, Klein is an advocate for instructing our schools on how to motivate students. He has given his time, working closely with teachers and administrators, to teach leadership, time management, communication and teamwork skills. He has also given back to his profession by working with and serving as the president of the Sales & Marketing Executives of Dallas.

The diversity of Klein's expertise, as well as his constant focus on personal development, created *Sell When You See the Whites of Their Eyes!*